You STiLL Can't Eat! Mt. Rainier!

BY

WILLIAM C. SPEIDEL, JR.

Illustrated by

BOB CRAM

Nettle Creek Publishing Co.   Vashon, Wash.

Printed and bound in the United States of America
by
Seattle Printing and Publishing Company, Seattle, Washington

DEDICATION

This book is being written with the late Neal Tourtellotte in mind . . . partly because he was the best Santa Claus the Children's Orthopedic Hospital ever had . . . partly because he probably never had a book dedicated to him and would have enjoyed it—but mostly because he got a great kick out of good food and good stories about people, and by writing "to" Neal we think we made this a better book.

"You Still Can't Eat Mt. Rainier"
(Come Now!)

Six years ago, we published a book with the improbable title, *"You Can't Eat Mt. Rainier!"*

To our delight ten thousand people purchased it . . . and since that there has been a constant demand for a sequel.

The idea for the original title stemmed from an episode in my father's life. Before he became a physician, Dad played baseball for a semi-professional club that went broke in British Columbia. He and Bill Kaysen were returning to Seattle on one of the sternwheel Kootenay River boats. They had 50-cents between them . . . a sum of money that represented either a night's lodging or a meal.

Bill was for the meal. Dad was for the night's lodging. In an attempt to take Bill's mind off of food, Dad pointed out the beautiful scenery. Bill's classic retort was, "Yeah, but you can't eat that!"

Mt. Rainier is our number one piece of landscape, so we take our title from it in pointing out that while we have grand scenery in the Pacific Northwest, there are many other things to do besides looking at it . . .

Hence the title for our new guide book to our city . . . including dining and the many other sides of Seattle.

vi

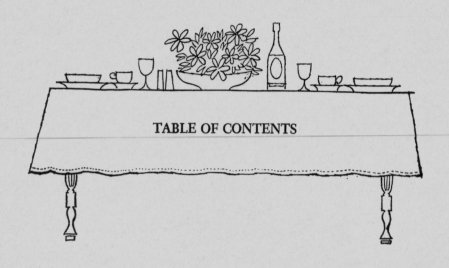

TABLE OF CONTENTS

Part I

Page

in which we paint the portrait of a city.

Pride and Prejudice............................. 3
Our Fathers Who Art . . . In Heaven?............ 6
Famous Fights................................. 26
Milestones 36
Sinews Of A City.............................. 44

Part II

in which we consider methods of taking advantage of Seattle

About "Faces"................................. 59
Shopping 78
After Dark.................................... 88
Do It Yourself Entertainment.................. 97
Pacific Northwest Food........................103
As A Matter of Facts..........................114

Part III

in which we take you on mouth-watering dining adventures

Restaurants 123

PART I

in which we paint the
portrait of a city

1

PRIDE AND PREJUDICE

It is virtually illegal to write a story about Seattle that does not include a four-color picture of sailboats on Lake Washington, with the Floating Bridge and Mt. Rainier in the background.

But that isn't Seattle. It's just the setting.

There are a thousand places on Puget Sound where pictures of sailboats with Mt. Rainier as a backdrop could be taken. There are a dozen magnificent geographic locations on the Sound for a great metropolis—and don't think everybody wasn't trying to make his location that city in the early days.

But Seattle is the one that emerged as the most important city of the northwest twenty-five per cent of the United States.

Why?

I've tried to find a more "genteel" way of expressing it, but nothing has withstood the succinct accuracy of the comment by one of our present-day leaders. And at the risk of having my Seafair pin stripped from my coat lapel, I will quote him verbatim:

"Why is Seattle the top dog? That's simple, son. We had more . . . and bigger . . . better *bastards* than the rest of 'em!"

Seattle is made up of "doers", don'ters", "doubters" and "deadheads". The don'ters make the doers so mad they accomplish the impossible. The doubters stay around to watch the doers fall flat on their faces.

The other 99% of the population doesn't even know anything is happening, but we need them around for bulk.

So when we refer to the Seattle Spirit, we're only talking about 1% of the population.

The California and Alaska gold rushes reveal a significant characteristic of our "one percenters". Many of them shook their shackles back in Ohio and Illinois because of the California gold rush in '49. But they didn't go for the big gamble of finding gold. They either worked in supplementary businesses that guaranteed a profit at the end of each week . . . or they veered up here to the less spectacular but more solid business of making small pieces of wood out of large ones.

In the Alaska rush, three quarters of Seattle's population caught the fever and "rushed" . . . but not our "one percenters." They stayed here and reaped their profits through merchandise and land speculation.

It is said of our pioneers that when it came to money, they were "tighter than Swiss watches". This picture has not materially changed in the ensuing years.

We're proud of the fact that (to date anyway) we're the youngest major city in the United States. It bothers us some that much of our greatness is due to dumb luck. Gold was discovered in quantity in Alaska nearly 30 years before the gold rush. Had the discovery taken hold at that time we would not have been equipped to handle the crowd.

It is slightly incredible to us, but time and again we've had the right man at the right time in the right place in our history —and all too often he was more interested in doing a good job than in making money. It bothers us that many of today's fortunes were made possible by loans from our leading prostitute during the panic of 1895.

We're proud of our year-round greenery . . . and we can't understand why a group of musicians would call themselves the

"Rainy City Jazz Band". We don't like the bad press on our precipitation. We like to think we *Keep Washington Green* through the activities of University of Washington students who keep his statue that color—as a prank—by painting it with green paint every February 22.

We're beginning to understand the kind of artistic people who have made us one of the major cultural centers of the United States, but among the descendants of pioneers, who didn't get around to a legal hanging for 30 years after we settled the place, this hasn't been easy.

We have taken to heart the admonition given to high school students in 1893 by James J. Hill, "If you want to know whether you are destined for success or failure in life, you can easily find out. The test is simple and infallible. Are you able to save money? If not, drop out; you will lose. You may not think so, but you will lose as sure as you live. The seed of success is not in you."

Yet, on a rare occasion, we are capable of shoving all our chips (or at least a reasonable percentage of them) on a big gamble if it looks like it will pay off. We put $100,000 to make up the difference when the Northern Pacific gave Tacoma a 50-cent-a-ton differential on wheat . . . we pledged an equal amount to get the Battleship Nebraska built here (although we ducked paying the pledge when it came to payment). We shoved plenty of chips out to publicize Seattle as the "outfitting" spot for the Alaska gold rush . . . the Alaska-Yukon-Pacific Exposition, and now Century 21.

* * *

And now, before I go on . . .

There are certain things that a Native Son must include in any history of our city. They have been stated so often that the entire population can recite them in unison. I list them in the most painless possible manner I can think of:

It was a rainy November 13 when a "hardy little band of pioneers" settled Alki Point.
Rolland Denny was weaned on clam juice.
Some Indians attacked us but we repulsed them.
C. D. Boren and "Doc" Maynard "gladly" gave Yesler land for a mill.
We were built on seven hills, like Rome.

5

We had a fight with a railroad and started our own.
Asa Mercer brought a lot of unmarried girls here.
We had a big fire.
The "Ton of Gold" story was important.
We had some riots about some Chinese.
We're named after an Indian who didn't like being "named after".
There is a 42 story skyscraper that is higher than most.
We're the *Queen City* of the *Evergreen State*.
We have a large company which makes things that fly.
When a gambler shot the chief of police, a jury acquitted him.
There is a lot of water around, including one large lake.
We're near a large mountain.
A lot of us own our own homes.
We don't like dogs.
We like flowers . . .

"Our Fathers Who Art . . . In Heaven?

"The noble army of courageous, enduring, persistent, progressive pioneers . . . (who had) the knowledge, foresight, faith and force that proclaimed them endowed with the genius of conquerors . . . thrifty, wise, faithful and far seeing . . .

"The wrench of parting with friends (back home) made a deep and lasting wound; no doubt every pioneer of the Pacific

Coast can recall the anguish of that parting whose scars the healing years have never effaced . . ."

The above excerpts are from a book by Emily Inez Denny, daughter of one of the members of the little band of pioneers who founded Seattle.

I have no doubt Miss Denny expressed an honest opinion, but there has been a general tendency to overlook the fact that the wounds some of our founding fathers acquired were more materialistic than those mentioned by Miss Denny.

They came from the guns of a sheriff's posse in hot pursuit.

There also has been a tendency to overlook the fact that most of our pioneers left home because they weren't making as much money as they wanted and thought they could make a million dollars out here . . . that they wouldn't have been "seen dead" with the kind of people we've been teaching our children they were.

They were robust . . . strong-minded . . . and oftentimes unscrupulous people who wouldn't otherwise have succeeded.

We in Seattle suffer from a set of strange psychoses that govern our lives in a subtle manner and help to make our city what it is. John Gunther put his finger on the problem when he was turning out one of his "Insides" and likened San Francisco to a "mistress" and Seattle to a "wife".

This bothers us on two fronts: We either know this isn't true and suffer from the hypocrisy of pretending that it is . . . or we think it is true but are afraid we aren't measuring up to the sterling qualities of antecedents who apparently were antiseptically pure.

One friend says it all began in 1909. At that point, he declares, a terrible wave of respectability swept over the city that was worse and more infectious than the influenza epidemic of 1918. Another acquaintance makes the point that San Francisco wrote its rascals into its history at a time when Seattle was busily writing her rascals out.

I believe it stems largely from the histories of Seattle that were written in that general period. Hoping it won't jar the descendants too much, we must first of all face the fact that it

7

was the custom of the day for history books to be financed by the people whose names appeared in them.

Also, these books had pictures of some pretty stiff-backed old codgers who, for the most part, were in the declining years of their lives. This causes us to overlook the fact that the oldest man who participated in the founding of Seattle was "old" Doc Maynard (usually referred to with the "old" written in as part of his name). Well, Old Doc Maynard was tottering along at the ancient age of 44 years when he landed in Seattle . . . after unceremoniously dumping his previous wife and children in Ohio without fretting about the troublesome details of a divorce.

"Old" Henry L. Yesler rates as the next oldest old timer. He was 42. Arthur A. Denny, who seems to us to be older than anyone else in the founding party because he really does represent the epitome of respectability, was a decrepit 30 years old. Most of the rest were in their 20's or 30's.

Needless to say, there was plenty of life in those "old boys" yet, when they set about founding our city. But how come this group was more successful than the pioneers of other communities?

Looking at it from a geographical standpoint, there's no reason why Port Townsend shouldn't be the San Francisco of the Northwest and Seattle the Oakland. I find no reason, either why Tacoma shouldn't be our major city. In fact, I find many reasons why Tacoma should be.

The facts are simply that our pioneer forefathers were just as tough as the rascals San Francisco boasts about—and a lot tougher than the fellows around us that were trying to make *their* city the number one in the Pacific Northwest. If not, we wouldn't have emerged on top.

There's something called "The Seattle Spirit" that's been peddled to us since childhood as the reason that we are on the top of the pile. I am not sure how it is defined currently, but as near as I can tell from research, the bonafide, original Seattle Spirit consisted of fighting among ourselves so murderously on an every-day basis that our claws were well sharpened and we were in fighting trim to band together when someone from the outside tried to move in on us and push us around.

Perhaps this approach is irreverent, but I like it fine . . . and it is in this vein there follow a few vignettes of the kinds of personalities we find among our founding fathers. To give you a quick cross-section, I've selected Henry Yesler, who was the Boeing of his day; Dr. David S. Maynard, who really put the original city together and as far as I can tell was the only one with a sublime sense of humor; Judge Thomas Burke, who helped get us both money and railroads; Jacob Furth, who was the real "boss" of the city for about 25 years; and R. H. Thomson, who not only created the physical profile of the city as it is today, but also successfully prevented any individual or group of individuals from putting the city in their own pockets for their own private benefit . . .

And then, for good measure, a sideglance at a few people who assisted the founding of our city on a more un-official basis . . .

"Seattle is a one-industry town. What will happen to our economy if Henry Yesler's mill burns down?" C. D. Boren 1854

It is significant of our collective personality that Henry L. Yesler took his inspiration from an acre of onions. Henry was our first industrialist, our first millionaire, and owned the first hotel, restaurant, department store, bank, post office, pier, water system—whatever it was, Henry had it first. We've named a street, library, and housing project after him.

The site of his original endeavor is around First and Yesler (now known as Pioneer Square) because that's where the tide lapped the shore in the early days. He employed everybody in town, including the Indian our city was named after. He made an industry click at a time when Wm. Renton* was losing his shirt in the same business at Alki Point and old Doc Maynard packed a thousand barrels of fish that turned rotten before they reached their market in San Francisco.

Yesler was jarred loose from Ohio by the 1849 Gold Rush in California. But his personality is reflected in the fact he became more interested in the success of a man who made $10,000 in one year by planting and retailing an acre of onions near San Francisco than he was in the progress of Mr. Sutter in the gold fields.

Yesler, who is cited as the "real" father of Seattle, had an asset hitherto unknown in the Pacific Northwest, and one that

Renton went on to build the biggest sawmill in the world at Port Blakely.

9

gave Seattle its first real leg-up on the rest of the communities. He had the knowledge and equipment for sawing a straight board in an area that was to be built on the strength of making small pieces of wood out of big ones.

He also had a stolid brand of cunning and cupidity that enabled him to make the most of it.

At the risk of annoying some of our readers in order to illustrate the character of our town, it is necessary to explode one of our favorite myths. The myth is that C. D. Boren and D. S. Maynard, who had laid claim to the center of our present city, were happy to "give" Yesler a lot of land in the interest of brotherhood and to provide the birth of the "Seattle Spirit".

It is a reflection of the Seattle Spirit all right, but it is doubtful that the word brotherhood should have been included. Yesler arrived at a time when half of our brave little band of settlers was determined the city should be along Alki Point, and the other half was equally determined it should be where it is now.

As a pure business matter, Yesler staked himself a couple of claims at the mouth of the Duwamish River, then more generally known as the "Duwumps." He was completely cognizant of the fact that the city would be built where the straight boards were being manufactured. (It is interesting to note that Yesler first chose a site close to the one now occupied by the Boeing Company.)

Yesler then made a proposition to Maynard and Boren that had the beautiful simplicity of a lot of our business propositions today. He diffidently suggested that he liked the name "Duwumps" for the potential city, an idea that was repugnant to Maynard, who was dead set on naming the city after his Indian friend, Sealth. And Yesler pointed out rather logically that Maynard's and Boren's claims would have a greater speculative value if they were north and south of a sawmill that could saw straight boards.

Under this dual brand of pressure, the two gentlemen "gladly" gave Yesler 320 acres in the heart of the city . . . a chunk of real estate that ultimately averaged out at $100,000 an acre and added considerably to Yesler's net worth.

Yesler was a shrewd gambler in the days when gambling was a less complicated method of getting rich than it is today.

Anybody that could do his holdings any good, like Wells Fargo and the Post Office, got free rent. He also found that holding public office was profitable.

When Henry was 80 years old he endeared himself to the local newspapers and the gossips by marrying 20 year old Minnie Gagle. But this was nothing compared to the material he provided on these two fronts a couple of years later by dying.

The provisions of Yesler's will were made known to a close friend about a week before the elderly gentleman became past history. According to them, Mrs. Minnie (as she was affectionately known in the press) was about to get a nice $20,000 in cash to build a house on Lake Washington and the income from the National Bank of Commerce building. The city which Yesler "fathered" was about to come into a grateful $100,000.

Unfortunately, after Henry's death, the will could not be found. This understandably upset the city fathers of the time and Mrs. Minnie and a couple of doctors were arrested and charged with feloniously destroying the will.

If the people of today would pause to consider that this was happening to the wife of our first millionaire, a man who had been mayor twice and had served in every public office except governor, some idea of the impact on the community may be reached.

The newspaper reporters of the day were somewhat more informal than they are today, and the story I thought was the most casual on the microfilm at the Seattle Public Library said in part, "we're selling papers as fast as we can get them off the press and the newsboys, the brave little fellows, are making a killing!"

A sadly-depleted Yesler estate ultimately went to Mrs. Minnie and some of the other deserving relatives. Mrs. Minnie disappeared from the scene. The city never got its $100,000.

But we really shouldn't complain. In a country where everyone else is blind, the man who can see is king. And in a lumber country where only one mill can saw straight boards, the major city is born.

11

The "odd-ball" . . .

There's always an oddball in the crowd, and "Old" Doctor David S. Maynard filled the niche with our bunch. *He* was 44 years old!

Everybody else came here for money. Doc came for love. He not only didn't take the usual route of an Indian mistress, he married the girl, a widow he met on the wagon train coming west. "Old" Doc also bewildered the rest of the fellows by having a sense of humor. And he needed that asset about 20 years after his arrival when some of his enemies brought a dreadfully legal first wife out from Ohio, and Doc had to do the honors in introducing Wife I to Wife II.

Doc was a little annoyed at the mayor of Olympia (wife II's brother) because the latter had run him out of town at gunpoint. So when the gentleman's son eloped with his 13-year-old sweetheart, Maynard had the girl put two pieces of paper marked "18" in her shoes and told a skeptical minister she was "over 18".

There was another thing the rest of the boys couldn't quite grasp about Old Doc. He was a Democrat. When they weren't looking, he sneaked down to the territorial capitol and got our county named after William Rufus King, a prominent Democrat who probably never heard of this section of the country and died enroute to taking office as Vice President of the United States.

Old Doc named all of the streets in his plat, south of Yesler, after all the Democrats he could find. This distressed the others so much they named theirs after Republicans. And when they ran out of names they resorted to calling one of their streets "Republican".

Doc wanted all the streets to run north and south. The others wanted to follow the contours of the bay. And that's why we've got a fair mess-up in our streets between north and south Seattle at Yesler Way today.

Maynard was a doctor . . . lawyer, and merchant chief, but he died broke. And even in death his timing was poor. He'd headed a campaign for a new cemetery, but died before it was dedicated and they had to keep his remains in a woodshed for a few days until a "decent" burial was possible.

Nevertheless, without Dr. Maynard who put the arm on

Chief Seattle for our name, we probably would have been called Duwumps, Washington, which we think would be a hell of a place to put a Space Needle . . . Duwumps.

He was much beloved, if not generally understood, by his compatriots. And we have a hospital and street named after him.

* * *

"What's good for the Great Northern Railroad is good for Seattle"—Judge Thomas Burke, 1892.

The above statement could perhaps in his day have been paraphrased, "What is good for Thomas Burke is good for Seattle." Fortunately, it worked out this way, and there is no question that Judge Thomas Burke made a major contribution to the character of our city.

However, he was not entirely a hero to the fellow citizens of his day. Chroniclers have pointed out that he didn't have to spit on his fingers to find out which way the wind was blowing.

One points out that Burke was not inclined toward "unprofitable idealism" . . . and that he possessed an enviable faculty for keeping his principles in harmony with his self-interest. It is interesting to note that he came here as a Roman Catholic and Democrat. He ended up as a Congregationalist and Republican. He also married the boss's socially-prominent daughter.

The following newspaper item, in the more outspoken manner typical of Burke's day, gives us a clue to the feelings he provoked in some of his fellow citizens:

"Ye Gods and little fishes, read the utterances of Judge Tommy Burke at the Citizens' League Tuesday evening. He cries 'stop thief'. To those familiar with the actions of the judge in the past and his manipulations of former nonpartisan and Citizens' League Councils, it will indeed be laughable. He says: 'The City of Seattle will never have its affairs honestly and economically managed so long as she permits political parties to choose her officers. The Industry and Commerce of the city cannot afford to be handicapped.'

13

"Very clever indeed, Judge. Dollars to doughnuts you have another franchise you want to railroad through a Citizens' League Council."

On the other hand, there is a monument to Burke in a park, there was a building named after him, and a street. And now there is a memorial museum being built in his name on the University of Washington campus.

Burke was local counsel for the Great Northern Railroad and as such he threaded the bringing in of a railroad through the intricacies of city politics. He also had a faculty for bringing in eastern capital, the *sine qua non* for the development of our raw territory.

He was founder of the Seattle Chamber of Commerce and willing to turn some of his money to civic purposes. Generally, he reflected the leadership of his day and ours in his statement, "You can't do much for the city if you haven't got money yourself."

He reached his peak, I think, as one of our pioneers, when he actually risked his life on the side of law and order during the riots against the Chinese.

A major volume on Burke, entitled "He Built Seattle", has recently been completed by Robert C. Nesbit. (I commend the book to you for an accurate, honest and detailed history of Seattle as it evolved from a town into a city.) Nesbit points to the following rather begrudging quote from an old issue of Olympia's *Washington Standard,* as an example of the kind of comment evoked about Burke and men similar to him. It was written at a time when Seattle was booming and the rest of the towns on Puget Sound were in the doldrums.

"These results are the natural sequence of well-directed industry, which has inspired a confidence that loosens the purse strings of the capitalists.

"Now the question arises, why is it that Seattle should be the point where all such enterprises enter? Is it because the facilities presented are better than those of other places on the Sound? Has Seattle any advantage not possessed by Olympia for the development and support of business projects? If she has, we fail to see it."

We can see it today, though. We had guys like Burke.

"*Jacob Furth was Seattle's last real banker*"

There are no statues, streets nor bronze plaques commemorating the job that this pioneer forefather did to make Seattle what she is today. And the people who know the true story of Furth's role in the transition of Seattle from a town to a city are not getting any younger.

We should by rights change the name of First Avenue to Furth Avenue.

He was the benevolent boss of the city for nearly a quarter of a century during her worst growing pains. In the panic of the 90's when fortunes were crumbling throughout the Pacific Northwest, Furth saved the day for more people than we will ever know about. And when his bank wouldn't make the loan, he sent many a deserving man to Lou Graham, who would lend the money if the man was recommended by Mr. Furth.

Lou was the city's leading "madam".

After the big fire in 1889, Jacob Furth and Angus MacIntosh—a Jew and a Scot—produced lower interest rates than the city had ever experienced, so we could build again. In 1895 when the board of directors of his bank demanded that as president he foreclose, he demanded two weeks in which to dig up additional capital.

He went to New York and obtained enough not only to keep his bank going, but to keep the rival banks in the city alive— and to hold our economy up until the Gold Rush of 1897 really pulled us out of the hole.

15

As one of Furth's contemporaries said, there was no law preventing a man from running for city office without consulting Mr. Furth. On the other hand if you wanted to *win* . . . *then* you consulted Mr. Furth before you filed.

Coast Magazine of the time did some imaginary interviews with potential candidates for the city council. In the fictitious interview with Furth, he was quoted as saying, "Why should I run for one position on the council when I already run the whole council?"

Furth occupied an office in the Pioneer Building at First and Yesler. He granted interviews with anyone needing money to get an enterprise going. He sized his man up in about 15 minutes. As he pointed out at one time, "Nobody had any collateral. We couldn't build unless we had faith in the people."

It is typical that when the city of Boston raised a million dollars for the victims of the San Francisco earthquake Jacob Furth was the man on the Pacific Coast entrusted to the wise expenditure of that money in the stricken California city. When a multitude of independent transit systems were going broke in Seattle, it was only Jacob Furth who could knock together the heads of the individualists who owned those systems and create a consolidated system.

Mr. Furth's calm confidence was illustrated after his death in the longest obituary I ever saw in the Seattle Times. It reported that Furth backed up to a hot stove with his hands behind his back, seriously burning him. He stepped away with calm deliberation, saying, "My, that stove is hot!"

That Mr. Furth could make mistakes was borne out by his financial encounter with L.S.J. Hunt, after whom Hunt's Point is named. Mr. Hunt came here as plain Leigh Smith, but felt the longer title was more appropriate.

At a point when Mr. Hunt needed money and Mr. Furth would not provide it, the former gentleman left his creditors, his city and his country. He proceeded to make another fortune in Egypt.

After the statute of limitations had run out, Mr. Hunt returned and paid all of his creditors in full—except Mr. Furth.

16

"R. H. Thomson, the man who never made a mistake"—See "That Man Thomson" by R. H. Thomson, U.W. Press, 1950

To me it is a sublime and significant thought in view of some of the engineering projects around our city today that the greatest city engineer Seattle ever had was not an engineer at all . . .

He was a Doctor of Philosophy.

As such he was suspect by the professional engineers, and it was his delight to believe they were "after" him, for in his autobiography he is at great pains to "chapter-and-verse" the number of times he confounded the professional engineers.

But the professional engineers were just sort of a "snack" to Thomson alongside of the selfish individualists who couldn't care less about what happened to Seattle as long as they got theirs.

And it is a mild bit of understatement to point out that Mr. Thomson was intensely energetic, shrewd, self-confident and fantastically important in shaping the physical character of our city as you see it today.

The Northern Pacific Railroad used as a rather reasonable excuse for not making Seattle its terminus the fact that we had a pretty hilly piece of landscape. Mr. Thomson caused those hills to be removed so we could get to Rainier Valley, to Mt. Baker, to Ballard and a lot of other places. He caused the hills to be washed down to create industrial property in all of the area south of King Street (the depot), which was the city's southern boundary when he arrived here.

Single handedly, he laid the foundations for the best supply of pure water at the least cost of any city in the world. At a time when Seattle desperately needed rail connection with the East he persuaded James J. Hill we would have a better city if the Great Northern would tunnel under the city instead of cutting it in half as the present engineers are now doing with the freeway through the heart of our city.

A maneuverer of Machiavellian proportions, he pushed through many improvements such as bicycle paths that now represent our system of boulevards . . . the initiative that created our city parks when a recalcitrant city council refused to put the question to a vote of the people.

He helped "found" City Light (our municipally owned electric system) . . . envisioned the harbor of Seattle where it is today and pushed for it. His prophetic judgment was such that he spent nearly three years finding the proper outfall for our city sewage system. Now, more than 56 years later, that outfall is going to be used by our $135 million metropolitan sewer system.

Mr. Thomson survived vigorous efforts to have him removed following the election of 7 mayors. He remained in office 20 years to the intense disappointment of a number of people. I recall one statement he made in the newspapers at a time when he was vigorously washing down our hills. "Seattle lies on the operating table with gaping, ugly, open wounds. But this surgery is necessary if she is to survive as a great metropolitan city."

And I can't resist one small anecdote that illustrates "that man Thomson" in action.

In anticipation of our needs for a water system, Mr. Thomson had ordered some $44,000 worth of assorted pipe from England. A British ship bearing this cargo was riding in the bay. Mr. Thomson also desired $86,000 to unload and lay the pipe.

The city comptroller felt the pipe was about three sizes too large and too expensive for the need and so informed the city council (or board of aldermen at the time). Alderman Carle was the key to the problem.

Now that the situation is established I introduce Mr. Thomson and how he handled the problem:

"The next day I met Alderman Carle on the street and told him I had a dream of his nice home place up on the slope. And whilst I was enjoying the view, I saw a grass and brush fire coming towards his house driven by a hard wind. It was July and the grass was brown and dry. 'What harm did it do to my house?' he asked. 'I'm sorry,' I said, 'But I was so frightened, knowing that your water mains are only one-inch and your lead-in pipe is only three-quarter inch, that I ran away. I was still trying to get out of the way when I woke up."

Did he get the shipload of pipe?

Let's not kid one another!

Isaac I. Stevens—Hatchet Man

The first record I find of any planned national publicity about our city comes in 1860 from obstinate, opinionated and hard drinking Isaac I. Stevens, our first Territorial governor; discoverer of the route west used by the Great Northern Railroad (commemorated by Stevens Pass); and chief engineer in charge of dispossessing the Indians from their lands. Because of his military ability, there are many who believed he would have been chosen to head up the union armies instead of General Grant, had he not been killed in the Civil War too soon.

Stevens, who had tramped from Minnesota to Puget Sound, (and there is a report that in Montana he had to walk back and forth in a small area all night in a snowstorm to keep from being frozen), wrote glowingly of Seattle in a letter that was used effectively in Congress by the Northern Pacific Railroad and led to the belief that Seattle must become the western terminus.

Stevens' report was accompanied by excellent illustrations of a competent artist and found its way into national magazines. He wrote about the fertility of the soil, the beauties of the country and of the economic mileage for a railroad on the northern route. He compared Seattle and Benicia, California (near Oakland) and showed Seattle was nearer Chicago by 217 miles . . . nearer New York by 420 miles . . . Baltimore by 389 miles . . . and nearer even to Charleston, Savannah and Mobile.

Stevens' report found a most receptive audience in James J. Hill who had the notion of moving cotton clothing by the shortest, fastest route to the Orient before the anti-trust boys of the federal government moved in on him and busted him of this idea.

* * *

Erastus Brainerd . . . The Right Man at the Right Time

The greatest contrived publicity program in the history of our city was the one engineered and directed by the Chamber of Commerce through Erastus Brainerd. More gold from Alaska had been landed in San Francisco, and possibly even Portland than in Seattle.

The others listed the landings in terms of dollars. Brainerd had a brainstorm. He called the $500,000 in raw gold that arrived on the steamer Portland in 1897 a "Ton Of Gold". It was this phrase that captured the imagination of the world. Brainerd must have really "lived" at that period. Speaking from the standpoint of a publicity man, myself, he had the ideal situation . . . the idea, the imagination and the financing. He wrote letters for miners to send to their home town papers. He wrote news stories from which he wrote magazine articles from which he wrote more news stories. He squeezed his stuff into government bulletins. He got lots of "breaks", too. The staff of the Kaiser in Germany thought his package of publicity was a bomb and refused to open it. What a nice nationwide story *that* made!

He milked the gold story for all it was worth and he had an interesting human quirk working with him. Anybody willing to risk his life savings . . . willing to give up whatever security he possessed wherever he was, on a wild gamble in a cold and totally strange place like Alaska—anybody like that had to be superstitious.

So who would "outfit" in Portland, or San Francisco, or any place else—when the story that motivated him to move emanated from Seattle?

Our Fun-Loving Forefathers vs. Canada

I was stopped for exceeding the speed limit in British Columbia by a province patrolman some years back. He said, "I don't know how you do it down in Washington, but up here we obey the speed laws."

If there have been times when you are viewed with a degree of suspicion by our neighbors to the north, leave it to an outgrowth of opinion established there by the "gay games" played on them by our fun-loving forefathers.

In 1869 a "goodwill" mission from Seattle was preparing to visit Victoria. As a special treat Senator George Francis Train was asked to head the party. A few days before the scheduled departure, Senator Train announced that the party planned to "invade British Columbia, seize as hostages ten leading Englishmen there, capture Vancouver Island, establish an Irish Republic around which would gather warm-hearted Fenians enough to drive the English aristocracy from the continent."

On the day before the party's departure he sent the follow-

20

ing telegram to the *Victoria Columbian*: "Will arrive early tomorrow morning. Will lecture on downfall of England."

Inasmuch as the Fenian Society, seeking Ireland's independence, had been formed in New York just 12 years before, and the English were sensitive to this sort of thing, the Canadians did not respond to this dubious approximation of a prank in the manner that was intended.

The steamer *Hunt*, with the "goodwill" party aboard was met by the British gunboat *Forward*. The guns of the gunboat were leveled at the *Hunt*. The sailors on board were at battle stations. A second line of defense was supplied by heavily armed policemen on the pier.

The captain of the *Hunt* decided that an immediate departure was the better part of an attempted explanation. And the goodwill party forthwith returned to Seattle.

* * *

In 1891, with the completion of a railroad between Seattle and the Fraser River, the Canadians were treated to another example of the rough sense of humor that pervaded our fun-loving forefathers.

A ceremony, replete with flags, speaker's platform, band, speeches and everything that goes with it, was being held in Blaine where the two last spikes were being driven—one on each side of the border. The mayor of Blaine got a telegram signed by James G. Blaine, who was the U.S. Secretary of State at the time. Among other things, it expressed the hope that British Columbia would one day be a state of the American Union.

The telegram accomplished one thing. It created a sensation. As the entire Canadian delegation to the ceremony prepared to leave in a body, someone confessed that the telegram was a fake, cooked up at the telegraph office in Blaine as a joke. (Joke?)

* * *

Chief Seattle's Revenge—The Indian Wars, 1851-1961

When we gave Chief Seattle a couple of drinks and persuaded him to let us name our city after him, he was singularly unimpressed. In fact, he warned us that not only would he be restless in his grave unto eternity, but warned us of mani-

21

festations of it to come, which would be wrought by the work of his tribesmen throughout our city streets.

For some decades we have clung to one of our great inferiority complexes—a sense of guilt at what we did to the wild life and Indians when we first arrived. Articles and literature from other parts of the country poke these fires once in a while . . . but the ghost of Chief Seattle provides the best fuel.

Looking at it from his point of view, we muscled into his territory with all the gentleness of a bunch of Chicago gangsters. We hi-jacked the best view property and even utilized their women in "squaw houses" to finance Seattle's development of successful real estate speculations that made us fortunes.

For some 50 years we carried on smugly . . . noting that a cougar hadn't killed a chicken at 4th Ave. and Pike St. since 1890 . . . that cougars hadn't been seen playing in a school yard since 1891 . . . that the last black bear caught eating preserves in a home at 8th Ave. and Cherry St. (only a few blocks past the Olympic Hotel) had been dead from bullet wounds since 1893.

But it seems like the earliest "natives" have gotten restless again.

There was something about a bear in our Carkeek Park a couple years ago. Recently, Mountlake Terrace, which suddenly cropped up as one of our major city communities, was visited by a cougar. And only a few weeks ago, a porcupine strolled down Pine St., site of our big, beautiful department stores.

In our times, the Quinault Indians have gone on a rampage quadrupling the price of our favorite type of salmon. Furthermore, they have banned a bridge through their reservation on the ridiculous grounds that paper plates and beer bottles do not decorate the landscape.

And now we've got an uprising in our Pioneer Square, right where Henry Yesler first got his start.

We did cure the Indians of wearing smoked clam necklaces as sort of a portable seafood snack bar about a hundred years ago. (We didn't mind their taste in the clams, but we were shooting for a condensed city and nobody could come within a mile of them.)

The present problem, however, concerns the inexpensive brands of wine drunk by the Indians down in our "Skidroad" area near Pioneer Square. The odor permeates the heart of "Old Seattle" . . . and also some of the Indians. This offends the olfactory sensibilities of the delicate ladies who shop the area for cut-rate paint, second-hand goods, and like to drink beer at night in the joyous new places in that area that revive the spirit of the Gay Nineties.

While we have some wonderful Indian friends, they do not include the ones found sleeping it off on benches in Pioneer Square—in the very shadow of one of our city's most impressive totem poles, carved painstakingly by their Alaska brothers as a WPA project.

We thought we had outflanked the Indians in the first Pioneer Square skirmish recently when we removed the park benches they slept on. But things have changed. A hundred years ago when we legally murdered old Chief Leschi, all we had to do was name a park after him to assuage the angry feelings of the protestors.

But when a protest went up over removing the benches from Pioneer Square, nothing would do but we had to put them back. However, we ingeniously inserted arm rests every foot or two. There again, we reckoned wrongly about the fortitude of the American Indian. They're sleeping across the bars now.

And the ghost of old Chief Seattle triumphs again.

Perhaps we ought to take the advice of Henry Yesler. He wanted to call our city "Duwumps" in the first place. Let's call it that, put Chief Seattle to rest, and be on our way to uninhibited cosmopolitanism.

* * *

The "Empire Builder" . . . or God Damn Mr. Sherman

Everybody in Seattle accepts the title of the Great Northern Railroad's "Empire Builder" as it chugs into the station from the east every day with the same indifference which it gives to the cigarette with the dubiously effective pronouncement that "it's got it at *both* ends." (My father is a doctor and the connotation of that one requires a shot of penicillin).

Yet the Empire Builder "made" Seattle. And had it not been for a fellow named Sherman and those Anti-Trust laws, he

23

probably would have made Seattle the greatest port on the west coast.

James J. Hill handed emigrants a favorable rate for moving west, but it didn't seem economically-sound to move empty trains east. And when he got around to looking at the freight rates for lumber, they added up to 90c a hundred-weight. One of our lumbermen concluded "we couldn't do any business unless it was reduced to 60c and no railroad man in his right mind would cut his rate by a third."

Mr. Hill concluded the lumberman had lost his senses, cut the rate to 40c, which was laughable in railroad circles until the Great Northern really began to open up the territory and make a profit.

He effected a coalition of Great Northern, Northern Pacific and Chicago, Burlington and Quincy railroad lines. In combination with Japanese steamships and his own *Minnesota* and *Dakota*, the two largest cargo carriers in existence, he put U.S. cotton in Shanghai *197 days faster* than any other carrier. He rounded out his first cargoes with iron and flour.

The return ships were filled with silk, rice, bean oil, hemp . . .

All through Seattle.

By a vote of 5 to 4, the Supreme Court held the combine was an unlawful restraint of trade.

And what is in the mill right now—half a century later? A merger of the Great Northern . . . Northern Pacific . . . Chicago, Burlington and Quincy Railroad.

* * *

"Head! He has no head at all! His neck just grew up and haired out!"—The Argus, 1908.

The *Argus,* which was born in 1894 and is still going strong, was typical of the press of the 1890's, which in turn was a mirror of the robust forefathers—who were busily building a city and had no time for many of the amenities we observe today. Here are some quotes from its pages up to 1908:

"If downright stubbornness were statesmanship, President Cleveland would be America's greatest statesman."

24

Headline: "Chapin, The Money Changer—Boodlers In Office To succeed our present mistake, Mayor Ronald"

The *Argus* never referred to its competing publisher as anything but "that tramp from Labrador." Here's one of many such references: "The influence which the tramp from Labrador attempted to bring to bear as an issue through his insignificant, dirty, lying rag, *The Telegraph* was wafted to the breeze and fell to the earth with a dull, sickening thud—*The Telegraph* is the prince of liars!"

The chauvinistially-inclined *Argus* always explained that "Chicago is the Seattle of Illinois."

"Will some kindly-disposed person tell, if they can, why the inspired idiots of Tacoma insist on calling the beautiful Mountain after their dinky little city?" (Authors note: I'm kindly disposed, but a little late. The Northern Pacific instigated the campaign to rename Mt. Rainier, Mt. Tacoma, to publicize its terminus. The matter wasn't officially settled until 25 years later.)

Caption under a caricature of James Hamilton Lewis, our then U.S. Senator: "A prominent Vice-Presidential impossibility".

"Head! He has no head at all! His neck just grew up and haired out!" (—my, but I like that one.)

* * *

And, just for fun, here's the story of one of our fore-"mothers"

In 1892, Miss Ursula Juanita Unfug, who apparently had physical charms not necessarily indicated by the name Unfug, became the first lady in our state to get away with murder— legally.

Miss Unfug shot and killed her paramour, Thomas Henderson Boyd, an Olympia newspaperman, during the course of a disagreeable argument in their hotel room.

Miss Unfug told an all-male jury (there were no women jurors then) that she hadn't minded living in sin with Mr. Boyd, and the fact that he beat up on her periodically wasn't so bad. But when he proposed to utilize her charms for the purpose of blackmailing some of our more prominent and wealthy citizens, like the men on the jury, she drew the line.

25

When he threatened to force her into this course of action by physical violence she resorted to the only thing she could think of at the moment and shot him dead. The jury agreed that Mr. Boyd was "vile" and "bad" and needed this kind of a lesson. And Miss Unfug was acquitted.

* * *

Famous Fights

"What we want is a story about the fights the city had to make itself; the people who will read it are not concerned with the birthplace of any of the men who engaged in the fight, or how old they are now, or were at the times of their deaths. And also let us have one volume that will not be full of portraits of those who are willing to buy their way into it and of eulogy of those who are prepared to purchase it."—Jacob Furth, about 1912.

Seattle gained its present position of prominence because of a more virulent degree of cussedness than the other cities in the Pacific Northwest.

I find no geographic nor climatic difference between our city and any of the others. I don't believe the facts warrant a theory that we had a greater degree of brotherly love. I do believe there was an element of luck that attracted the fighters here.

At any rate, I think the fights then and now help us understand why we are a great city and why I believe we will continue as one. Only recently a member of our Chamber of Commerce provided a quote that I think underlies our philosophy. He said, "I know we should shake hands across the river and be friendly with Portland, but if you hang on to that too hard, you're liable to *drown.*"

First Day—First Fight!

Our first fight occurred the day the "hardy little band" of settlers arrived here . . . November 13, 1852. It took place between the husbands and wives.

It was raining. Some idiot had forgotten to bring a frow from Portland and there was no roof on the single establishment in the place. (To you easterners, a frow is an instrument with which you make shakes . . . like for shake roofs).

The women of the hardy little band were crying. They were of the opinion that the whole venture was a pretty stupid project. Unlike the housewives of today who are pestering their husbands to go "out" and eat, these gals had no place to eat but "out." And they went on strike. They refused to do the cooking.

With a forced cheerfulness, the men went about the business of cooking dinner outside and that's how they became stuck with being the barbecue cooks in the most barbecued backyard city in America.

The First Street Fight . . .

The next real fight came in about 3 months when half of the hardy little band realized that Alki Point, where the monument to the founding of the city still can be found, was no location for a city. The other half was of an equally fervent opinion that the original location would become the "New York" of the west coast.

City streets were platted and industries were started in both locations and there was absolutely no love lost between the opposing factions in the struggle for power . . . or perhaps it could be more honestly established that this was a struggle for greater profits in land speculation.

It is in character that businessman Yesler chose the present site of the city. Doc Maynard gave up his plat—everything

27

south of Yesler Way—to grow potatoes on an Alki Point farm, which he ultimately sold for $460.

Nice University, But No Students . . .

We got into a wonderful ruckus over the creation of the University of Washington. There was money to be had from the sale of state lands for the location of a university, and Daniel Bagley was the man who went after it.

The State Superintendent of Schools took the rather reasonable position that there was no one single human being in the state who was qualified by educational background to enter any university, but this kind of nonsense was brushed aside and we beat out the rest of the counties who were just as interested in getting that state land as we were.

Bagley talked Arthur A. Denny out of 8½ acres and C. C. Terry out of 1½ acres in a nice location where some years later we built our 1,000-room Olympic Hotel, the most important in town.

Bagley went about the business of selling off school lands at $1.50 an acre, which turned out to be in greenbacks and considerably inflated. There was quite an uproar when the other side hollered for an investigation of Mr. Bagley's lack of business acumen, but it was finally resolved that if you wanted to get things done you had to cut a few corners and we shouldn't bother too much about the details.

As things have turned out, Mr. Bagley was dead right. The University of Washington presently is Seattle's third largest industry and the present tenants of the original site of the University—Western Hotels and University Properties—pay the University $3,000,000 a year.

You Run Your Railroad Your Way . . . And I'll Run Mine Your Way.

Most present-day Seattleites are aware that some time in the distant past there was some kind of a ruckus between Seattle and the Northern Pacific Railroad. Few realize the struggle between the two opposing forces went along for 20 years.

The basis of the struggle was simple. The Northern Pacific was trying to kill Seattle off by naming Tacoma its western terminus.

28

One official promised one of our pioneer forefathers he would live to see grass growing in Seattle's streets.

This was not an attitude designed to produce self-abasement in our rowdy little town. Historians generally credit the Great Northern or the Gold Rush in Alaska with the building of our city.

I'm more inclined to credit the Northern Pacific and herewith state some of my reasons.

In effect, the Northern Pacific was a large land company building tracks between its pieces of property to make money on land speculation, not railroading. In some instances, such as in Yakima, where the townfolk moved their town four miles to be near the depot, this was a very profitable policy indeed.

But Seattle was a different proposition. The Northern Pacific was harassed with financial problems and other angry settlers across the nation, and Seattle was a hardy juvenile delinquent that kept kicking the big company on the shins.

The policy of the railroad was not exactly gentle. There was no such thing in the East, for example, as a ticket to Seattle. If an Easterner once got out here, he had to stay overnight in Tacoma because the railroad also controlled passenger boat transportation to Seattle. It cost 50c a ton more to get wheat into the Port of Seattle from eastern Washington than to those same facilities in Tacoma.

We, in turn banged away at the Northern Pacific by trying to have Congress remove the company's land grants.

And while we were highly resentful of the Northern Pacific's philosophy of life, we recognized there could be money in it and we copied it on a local basis. And *anything* which there could be money in was worth a college try as far as we were concerned.

Playing the same game as the Northern Pacific, we got control of the "Mosquito Fleet"—the little freight boats supplying the farmers around Puget Sound. We adopted the "transportation-land-speculation" formula on a local scale. We bought land in what is now Ballard, West Seattle and other outlying communities and built street car lines to our property. We didn't expect to make money on the street car lines, but we sure did on the land. In some places, like Ballard, this worked out fine. In others, like West Seattle, people went broke.

29

One of the stratagems employed by N.P. was that of offering free lots to people the company wanted in Tacoma. At one point, an embittered editorial writer in that city commented, "This policy brought the deadheads to Tacoma. The fighters stayed behind in Seattle to continue the fight."

The Battle between North and South—Canal, that is

Anyone interested in battle scars as they appear on our present-day landscape should take note of the large hole in Beacon Hill just south of Sick's Brewery.

That's where they first started digging the Lake Washington Ship Canal. The south canal was hooked up with filling in the tide flats, creating Harbor Island, etc. At one point nearly the entire town was whooping and hollering for the south canal. But a couple of old die-hards kept whacking at the present site through Lake Union. They won the battle when the news got out that in the south canal we would have to spend our money while with the north canal we could get Federal government money.

We fought for 60 years to get the ship canal. The publicly-stated reason for the canal was that ships of the world could go into Lake Washington, drop their barnacles and depart again unencrusted. I doubt if there are any barnacles at the bottom of Lake Washington and some of my friends in the ship-repair business have contributed to my delinquency in this respect.

The real idea was far more practical. The huge steel mill that was to make Kirkland the Pittsburgh of the Pacific Northwest needed water transportation for its piers to the ports of the world.

Fortunately, the dream of that mill is one of the little mistakes that men building a new country made. About a million dollars was spent building the mill. But its fires were never lit. Its doors never opened.

We wouldn't have been the lovely city we are today if that one had worked out.

A lot of boats go through the canal today. Over a million visitors a year trek out to see our Government Locks. But, I doubt if our forefathers would have gone to all that effort to cut the city in half for the benefit of the pleasure boats which comprise its main traffic today.

30

"If God is on our side, who can be against us?" Answer: *Tacoma*

Looking at things in the light of present day conditions, it is difficult to conceive of a situation in which either money, sewers or dogs (with the possible exception of sex) would not have a priority of our attention.

But I think it is some indication of our inner conflicts that the first three days of the constitutional convention by which we were preparing ourselves to become a state were occupied with none of the above questions. The problem that raged in our legislative halls concerned the question of whether or not God should be mentioned in the preamble of the constitution.

At the end of that time, the *P.I.* reported that "the forces of the Lord had prevailed and the enemy had been completely routed . . . "

The Lord plays a prominent part in our community. For example, most of us contribute rather handsomely to our churches. However, being the individualists we are, we see no need for attending church to prove to ourselves that we are a determinedly Christian people.

We would not exercise this same approach if we were training for a tennis match, but we generally are of the opinion that we can exercise Christianity without practicing it, just as we vote for "the man" in politics without knowing how our government operates.

However, there was one notable occasion in which the "Hand of the Lord" went to a referendum vote of the people. It is with considerable satisfaction that I point out that the Lord won in Seattle, but I am distressed to report He didn't do quite as well with a Tacoma jury. It cost the city of Seattle the biggest claim for damages it has ever paid.

Although R. H. Thomson, our most famous city engineer, went to his grave with the unalterable conviction that never in his lifetime did he make a mistake, even he must have wavered a little when he considered the question of the Boxley Canyon flood.

The beginnings of this problem date back a number of years to the time when there was 4,000 feet of ice over the

31

entire area, which is quite considerably higher than even the Space Needle. And though this simplification will grate the nerves of the technicians in geology at the University of Washington, some of this ice blocked off some canyons with porous glacial moraine.

Against the advice of geologists, the city built a dam for the purpose of storing Cedar River water and of producing electricity. The geologists pointed out one side of the dam was porous and might create problems.

The problems became quite serious. Water, rocks and such washed out the Milwaukee Railroad tracks December 23, 1918, and seriously damaged the operation of a North Bend sawmill.

The railroad took a run at the city via the legal route and a Seattle jury held the flood was an *Act of God.* The case with the lumber mill about the same question got into a legal entanglement over instructions to the jury. The city council felt that time and money could be saved—and this seemed satisfactory to the lumber company—if things could be settled out of court for $135,000.

By this time the citizenry had been aroused. The offer by the city council was forced by referendum to a vote of the people. In essence the question concerned whether or not the flood was an *Act of God* and *God* won 20,060 to 17,436 in 1925.

The lumber company attorneys, still clinging to their legal technicality, successfully made the point they couldn't get a fair trial in King County after that vote. The matter was referred to a Tacoma jury which pleasurably returned a judgement in favor of the plaintiff to the tune of $361,867.81.

The War Between the States—Wash. and Ore., That Is

The last outbreak of open hostility between the states of Oregon and Washington occurred on April 3, 1896 in the "Battle of Baker Bay" during which the Washington forces were completely routed.

The "invasion" of Washington was made by 200 to 300 Oregon fishermen, armed to the teeth and bent on destruction. They crossed the Columbia River and made an attack on the Washington fishermen. They tore out a fish trap, wrecked different pieces of property, set three pile drivers adrift. After

32

doing damage of about $1,500 and routing our fishermen, they warned the latter this was just an interesting sample of what they would do if our fishermen ever again attempted to fish in "their" river.

Washington's Governor McGraw called out the National Guard, which consisted of Captain Frank E. Adams, the hero of the occasion, a Lieutenant Skinner, 7 sergeants, 6 corporals and 28 privates from companies "D" "E" and "V", all of Seattle.

On April 9, our troops kissed their wives and sweethearts goodbye and entrained for Vancouver, Washington to establish encampments and patrols up and down the river night and day for 86 days. Hostilities were brought to a close when a Washington fisherman, arrested by an Oregon sheriff, appealed to our federal courts. District judges from Oregon and Washington jointly heard the case and reached the decision that the two state lines extended to the middle of the river and neither had jurisdiction beyond that point.

Captain Adams, under extremely trying conditions, kept anybody from shooting anybody else. In his report to the Governor after the fracas, the Adjutant General of our side stated the encounter was extremely trying to our men who were not hardened to the constant downpour of Oregon rain.

* * *

The Rhododendron—An All-Female Fight

Lest the impression be given that only the fighting qualities of our men gave Seattle supremacy, the story must be told about the battle over the naming of the rhododendron as the state flower.

In 1892, under a law passed by the legislature, the women of the state, and only the women, were authorized to select by ballot, the official state flower.

This resulted in a battle of tremendous proportions that was carried on in the newspapers, in booths at department stores and banks, torchlight parades and the like. Mrs. Elsora Heyner Frye, of Seattle, led the Rhododendron "Party". Mrs. Ella Higgins of Whatcom, led the Clover Forces.

Although Mrs. Higgins had established a "Fifth Column" in Seattle through Mrs. Kate Turner Holmes in the battle which

33

raged back and forth for six months . . . and although there were various "splinter" parties, the outcome of the vote was as follows, thanks to the superior tactical ability of Mrs. Frye:

The Dogwood, 34 votes . . . Marguerite 84 . . . Washington Holly (Oregon Grape) 227 . . .Gaillardia 730 . . . Clover 5,720—and the Rhododendron 7,704.

* * *

The Victory of the Crass-headed Idiots"

By stretching things a little, I suppose Seattle has a municipally-owned water system because nobody seemed to pay any attention to an ordinance passed by the city council in 1882 requiring tin roofs on all buildings except privies.

Seven years later a fire burned down practically every building in the business district. Presumably the sparks would have been less effective if anybody had paid any attention to that ordinance.

In those early and more boisterous days some of the leading citizens after whom parks, schools, streets, etc. are named, had put together a private water system at a cost of about $100,000. It was bringing them a nice return on their money —about $80,000 a year in round numbers, which were the kind of round numbers they enjoyed.

Mayor Robert Moran had the temerity in late 1888 to suggest that the folks be given an opportunity to vote on whether or not they preferred a municipally-owned water system. Our pioneer forefathers were old hands at manipulating things in City Hall and they stalled for six or seven months while they got around to figuring out how to create an indefinite postponement.

This large fire broke out on June 6, 1889. It really started as a comparatively small fire, but within about 20 minutes there wasn't any water coming out of the hydrants. The wooden roofs of the buildings were excellent targets for sparks. Historians guesstimate the loss at anywhere from $10,000,000 to $20,000,000.

The city council hastily put together an election on the question of public versus private ownership of our water system

34

and a month after the fire, with the hydrant matter fresh in their minds, the voters decided 1,875 to 51 in favor of the former.

This was only the beginning of the fight. The gentlemen who were losing that delightful return on their investment were not without influence. The *Post Intelligencer,* which joined up with the private water people, coined the term "crass-headed idiots" in referring to the public water people, and it stuck.

This fight was no Sunday School picnic The leading citizens had a bottomless campaign kitty. And the city was so broke as a result of the fire it couldn't finance its own system. Then somebody discovered that revenue bonds would not increase the general obligation of the city and the money could be had.

R. H. Thomson, who was the chief thorn in the side of private enterprise for about a quarter of a century, made an amazing deal with Judge J. J. McGilvra, who had sided in with the businessmen. McGilvra could submit his brief in favor of private water. Thomson would submit his brief in favor of public water. And McGilvra could be the judge of who was right.

A couple of weeks before the election on floating the bonds, McGilvra deserted his buddies, came out publicly for public water, financed the public water campaign—which just skimmed by a vote of the people.

Arthur A. Denny was so annoyed at his friend of 30-years standing that when he and McGilvra met on the street the next day Denny fired McGilvra as his attorney, announced he would never speak to McGilvra again and, as far as the record shows, never did.

Milestones

Seattle's Chamber Music...

Although not many people are aware of it today, the Lord had a lot to do with the formation of the Seattle Chamber of Commerce . . . that is, the Lord, Tacoma, the Northern Pacific Railroad, Port Townsend and the Portland Board of Trade.

James P. Ludlow, a Baptist minister by profession, desired to preach Christianity to the Indians around Puget Sound, but his work did require a little income, so he maneuvered himself into the government mail contract between Port Townsend and Sitka, Alaska.

Mr. Ludlow had a small steamer, the *Evangel,* with which he hoped to perform services for both the Lord and the Post Office Department. He also proposed to make his city, Seattle, the southern terminus for the mail. This was inimical to Portland, which previously had been the southern terminus and had the previous contract . . . to Port Townsend, which was resenting the lusty youth, Seattle . . . to Tacoma and the Northern Pacific Railroad because as far as they were concerned, Seattle should "drop dead".

There wasn't much question about the ability of the *Evangel* to minister to the religious needs of the Indians on Puget Sound. The matter of her seaworthiness on a trip from Sitka to Portland was a subject for serious speculation. And the United States steamboat inspectors who would do that speculating were stationed in Tacoma, within easy reach of influential people in that city and the Northern Pacific.

Judge Thomas Burke got advance information that the steamboat inspectors were going to "ding" the *Evangel* and chartered the tug *Mastick* on Ludlow's behalf. But the men realized this was only a temporary expedient . . . that other cities were always "ganging" up on Seattle. The city needed a free-wheeling organization that didn't have to pay as much attention to the Marquis of Queensbury rules as the official city government.

So on April 17, 1882, twenty-three of the fellas got together and formed the Seattle Chamber of Commerce.

A resolution taking a roundhouse swing at the Portland Board of Trade was the first order of business. The gist of the resolution was that we formally and strenuously protested the action of the Portland Board of Trade in attempting to have the Ludlow contract annulled. It was called an "unwarranted intermeddling with a matter which in nowise concerns it." We further pointed out that after careful inquiry and investigation, it was clear Mr. Ludlow had the ability and was ready with the most ample facilities for the transportation of the mail in accordance with the requirements of the contract.

It turned out we were a little over-resolute because neither the *Evangel* nor the *Mastick* was capable of carrying the mail and the contract was turned back to the former Portland carrier. But we didn't bleed too hard because we had kicked up so much of a fuss that Seattle, not Portland, was named the southern terminus for mail from Alaska.

In a more recent ruckus, the Chamber was a leading force in causing the main Pacific Northwest Post Office facilities to be moved from Portland to Seattle. And the Chamber is currently engaged in a fight to eliminate a freight rate differential between eastern Washington and the coast, a matter in which Portland presently has the edge.

* * *

"What Seattle Needs Is A Good Fire"
—Anon., 1962

I have mentioned before it is not permitted that a Native Son write a story about Seattle without also including a mention of the GREAT FIRE of June 6, 1889.

Although Fire Chief Fitzgerald has one of the finest fire-loss records in the country and would definitely frown on such a proposition, there are those today who believe that "what this city needs is another good fire."

The big fire enabled us to widen our streets, knock out humps and hollows and start with some dandy new buildings. On the other hand, there are some interesting sidelights that don't generally crop up on the surface that seem to me interesting enough to record.

I'm a great admirer of the Tacoman who hired every baker in Tacoma to stay up all night the night of the fire to supply us with fresh rolls along with our ashes the next morning.

The fire moved about 100 yards an hour, there being no wind . . . About 7 o'clock in the evening it reached Yesler Way and the choicest part of the city (if you were a fire) where the densest portion of the buildings existed. From 7 p.m. on it was something that Nero would have loved.

For two weeks a Tacoma tent, financed and manned by people from the city, provided food and lodging for thousands of destitute persons. Some of our richest pioneers, who were at the time building mansions befitting their business positions, lost both their businesses and their fine homes—permanently. The parents of Alice B. Toklas, Gertrude Stein's "friend", lost $400,000 when their drygoods store went up in smoke.

A couple other cities in the state had fires that year, but, as usual, Seattle was the *firstest with the mostest* and grabbed all of the national publicity. Cash gifts from around the country amounted to $104,150. We got a lot of new citizens on account of the publicity—some of them on account of the cash. The latter rolled in for the purpose of such freeloading as was available in the relief tents.

The paid secretary of our relief organization succumbed to the temptation of improving his salary by mis-appropriating about $3,000—in addition to which he got 5 years of free room and board at the state penitentiary in Walla Walla, as a guest of the state.

I know the following are nothing but details . . . *details*. But some people might want to know what happened to the money that was left over after the economy of the city had ground back into regular gear and the Relief Committee went out of business.

Here's how: To Grace Hospital, $282.50 . . . The Women's Christian Temperance Association for the Children's Day Nursery $2,500 . . . To the Women's Home Association, $8,000 . . . to the Ladies' Relief Society, for its Orphan's Home, the remainder of $10,831.

Sixty four acres in the heart of Seattle were destroyed by the fire . . . every bank, wholesale house, hotel, newspaper office, both fire engine houses, most every store—and an estimated one million rats, but no people. About a mile of buildings . . . from University to King Street on First Avenue . . . from Spring to Yesler Way on Second Avenue . . . all railroad trestles along the waterfront, warehouses and mills . . . and all wharves except the one at the foot of Union Street. The cost ran somewhere between $10,000,000 and $20,000,000 depending on your source.

There is one major area in Seattle today listed by the insurance companies as a "conflagration area" . . . it's in the same general section where the original fire was the worst. Some people think a good fire would be a nice way of getting rid of it. The Fire Department, proud of its present record, is not enthusiastic about this philosophy . . . and the upper stories of many of these buildings have been vacated as fire hazards as one precaution of keeping this nightmare from coming true.

* * *

"I got a idea! Why not buy Alaska?"

There was virtually nothing that our pioneers wouldn't take a run at if they thought there was money in it, but I'll bet that even they didn't know how well they were going to score when the owners of Seattle's fishing fleet got mad at the Russian government in 1866 for not letting us use Alaska.

In that year, the fishermen's lobby in Olympia persuaded the Territorial Legislature to "memorialize" President Andrew Johnson with the following words:

"That abundance of codfish, halibut and salmon of excellent quality have been found along the shores of the Russian possession. Your memorialists respectfully request Your Excellency to obtain such rights and privileges of the Government of Russia as will enable our fishing vessels to visit the ports and harbors of its possessions to the end that fuel, water and provisions may be easily obtained; that our sick and disabled fishermen may obtain sanitary assistance, together with the privilege of curing fish and repairing vessels in need of repair. Your memorialists finally pray Your Excellency to employ such ships as may be spared from the Pacific Naval Fleet in exploring and surveying the fishing banks known to navigators to exist along the Pacific Coast from Cortez Bank to Behring Straits."

Just as an odd-ball suggestion accompanying the Memorial we asked the President to investigate the possible purchase of "Russian America".

The Memorial was handed to the Russian Ambassador who diffidently suggested that this piece of real estate just "might" be for sale . . . which it really was and which we bought a year later for $7,200,000 . . . which resulted in a Gold Rush 30 years later, the silver horde of salmon, the present pulp industry and the future oil industry all of which make up one of the main arteries of our city's economic circulatory system.

Just a little suggestion tacked on to a "beef" to the President of the United States but one of those little things that make us the most important city in our neck of the woods.

* * *

"How do you know she turned to stone?"

Someone once explained to me that a young city is like a young family—so busy making money for the necessities of life that it doesn't have much time left over for the niceties.

The case in point is illustrated by a casual comment made in one of the manuscripts of our history in connection with "Old Mother Damnable", or Mary Ann Boyer, who ran a boarding house on the east corner of First Avenue south and Jackson Street in about 1852. Mrs. Conklin crops up in all kinds of histories as a "character" because she was plain spoken, vulgar and usually extremely profane, earning her the Mother Damnable title, which was considered quite amusing at the time.

The casual mention goes like this: "It was found many years after her death that while lying in the cemetery her body had turned to stone . . ."

The question that immediately occurred to me was, "Why in the world would they be digging up Old Mother

Damnable so they could learn that her body had turned to stone?"

The whole thing boils down to a lack of city planning.

We were a young city growing so fast that we didn't know how to handle it—and nobody had heard about city planning a hundred years ago anyway. We were like a woman in a new house trying out her furniture this way and that to see which way it looked the best.

And that was our problem with cemeteries. We kept changing their locations. Lakeview Cemetery became the final resting place for some 223 bodies that had been in the old cemeteries. They were raised, as one historian puts it, "re-boxed and re-buried".

A substantial number of our old pioneers had received this treatment four times before they came to their final resting place and it was during one of these episodes that we learned Old Mother Damnable had turned to stone. P. T. Barnum tried to buy her body, but the contractor in charge coldly informed him he was in the business of transferring bodies. Selling them to a circus was not in his contract.

* * *

"Our Sacrosanct Wagon Train"

Perhaps there are those who will object to the inclusion of the "Willie Keil" story in this section on the grounds he isn't really a part of Seattle lore. On the other hand, if he had just happened to think of Seattle instead of Raymond, the monument would be here.

Besides, the story is too wonderful to pass up.

Willie wanted to start a "sect" settlement in Washington. Unfortunately, the Lord took Willie unto his bosom before the wagon train Willie headed could leave Ohio.

Willie's father, being a sentimental soul, caused the creation of a lead casket into which he put a barrel of good whiskey and the body of his son. The casket was placed in a hearse which headed the most unmolested wagon train in the history of the West.

Indians, sans arrows, knelt at the side of the trail in awe as the prairie ships of that particular project sailed through. And the state has seen fit to erect a monument commemorating the event.

41

Here are some miscellaneous milestones we're tossing in the pot just to give the stew a little added "body".

If your name is Thompson you may be able to successfully trace your lineage to John Thompson. And if your name is Baxter you may be able to trace out him as an ancestor. In 1880, Mr. Baxter interferred in a quarrel between two drunks and got stabbed to death as an important result of his action. He was stabbed by Mr. Thompson who has the distinction of being the first person legally hung in King County and the first white man hung in the territory. This very important event in Mr. Thompson's biography occurred at 1:30 p.m. on September 28, 1880.

* * *

Perhaps it might distress some chauvinistic Portlander to find out that the title "Queen City", the sobriquet that is applied to our city throughout the world, was coined for an advertisement in the Portland papers.

Credit for this name goes to a Portland real estate firm, Russell and Ferry, which was trying to make money on real estate speculation in Seattle in 1869. The firm had 1,500 acres for sale in what they called the future "Queen City of the Pacific". The name took hold and we've been plugging it ever since.

* * *

I am intrigued by the fact that in one of the first jury trials (1854), Luther Collins was awarded damages of one-cent. Court costs in the same case added up to $269.32. Mr. Collins was not pleased with the verdict.

* * *

We weren't the only ones who damaged the "poor Indians". Chief Kitsap, the son of the man for whom the county is named, met death in a violent fashion at the hands of his tribesmen.

It seems that the younger Kitsap was cured of an ailment at the Fort Steilacoom hospital by some red medicine, which he thought was red paint. He emerged from the hospital under the misconception that he was an important medicine man. When three of his braves got sick he fed them generous quantities of red paint, which caused their deaths. Their relatives fell upon Kitsap and killed him.

42

Governor Isaac Stevens, who was to say the least, a pompous little man—but effective—had the chore of officially dispossessing the Indians of their lands so that the white people could fight among themselves over the same real estate.

The apocryphal story is that Chief Seattle, a rather large gentleman, casually rested his hand on Stevens' head during his oration at the treaty-meeting where he was accepting the inevitable on behalf of his tribesmen. This, alone, should make us proud that our city is named after this Indian.

But Stevens wasn't half as mad at Seattle as he was a few years earlier when an Indian was murdered in his office. The Indian was being kept there over night because it was considered sort of sacrosanct and he would be safe there until he could be transported to Fort Steilacoom.

The governor didn't mind that the man's enemies sneaked in at night and murdered him. He was real upset, however, at the mess they made of the office during the process.

* * *

It is within my memory as a newspaper reporter—which places it in the last 20 years—that someone made the following comment about a county commissioner: "He's so crooked that when we bury him, we'll have to screw him into the ground."

The gentleman in question subsequently was retired to the state penitentiary in Walla Walla for a period of rest and relaxation.

We made a lot of noise about such things in the past, but we found it difficult to get downright mean about it when our pioneer forefathers were the culprits and the living was easy.

* * *

It's pretty hard to pin down the exact location, but the legislature in 1876 authorized the County Commissioners to build a jail for a price not to exceed $12,000. Our elected representatives purchased a site on a fractional half block between Jefferson and Yesler Way (which belonged to the "father of our city", Henry Yesler) for $3,500. The contract for the jail was $11,331, plus incidental expenses which brought the total up to over $16,000.

Did the grand jury summoned to probe the problem get so

43

stuffy as to send a loyal pioneer to the penitentiary? No. On the other hand, they were just a little critical of the entire operation. They pointed out that the commissioners had bought and paid for a piece of property to which clear title had not been obtained and on which there was a heavy mortgage.

The Commissioners also had spent $16,000 on a project on which they were only authorized to spend $12,000. And that furthermore the "jail" was so poorly constructed that "it would be a safe place for prisoners only if they were first secured with irons".

So nobody went to jail. In those days, it wouldn't have been cricket.

* * *

Sinews of a City

It was mentioned before that there is more to Seattle than some pretty sailboats on Lake Washington.

The material that follows indicates some of the interplay of forces that keep our city "in balance" and make it important.

Like most American cities where it is geographically possible, Seattle's growth has been to the north. Our "heart" once was down on Pioneer Square. It now has moved to more-or-less the area of the Metropolitan Tract (from the Olympic Hotel north to Pine Street).

We lowered Denny Hill—out toward our new Civic Center (Century 21)—as much as 109 feet or a ten-story building. And there were those who speculated in land (which has been the biggest money maker in Seattle's history—land speculation) on the bet the center of the city would move to this regraded area.

We've had the same flight to "suburbia" experienced by other major metropolitan cities. But a "balance" of forces has enabled us to peg the heart of our city. On another front, the interplay between the University of Washington, with its emphasis on "pure" theory, and the business of a major city, with its emphasis on "pure" practicality, have kept the situation dynamic but in balance.

Most of our "mainline" restaurants are downtown. We do our major shopping downtown. The financial heart of the city is downtown. Our major movies are downtown. Even an organization as all-powerful as Boeing has an employment office downtown.

* * *

Boeing . . . Boiiing!

There have been, are now and ever shall be millions of words written about the Boeing Company. I favor the following illustrative anecdote.

For some time, I had tried for an appointment with a very busy guy named Bill Allen, who started being president of this company when he was 45 years old. When the opportunity came, it came with a rush. I had 30 minutes in which to get from my office to his.

When I appeared before the rather formidable and security-ridden reception desk in the main lobby I informed a most gracious young lady that I had an appointment with Bill Allen. "Could you tell me what department he is with?" she asked.

A little bit diffidently, I said, "He's the president of the company."

This created a fair degree of red-faced fluster and the reply, "Oh dear, nobody has ever asked *me* to see *him* before!"

If you've never met him, I'm really quite sorry because he is one of the most unassuming possessors of a razor-like mind I have ever met and you would like him. My first question was, "Why is Boeing here?"

After about five minutes of silence on the part of Mr. Allen

I started to repeat the question and he retorted a bit sharply, "I'm *thinking* of the answer!"

By way of an answer Allen pointed to a copy of the company's annual report. Tossing it aside, he said, "It says we have net assets of $237 million dollars. But that isn't our wealth. Our wealth is the 'long-hairs', and they like living here."

(It is reported that Boeing has the greatest pool of engineering talent in the world. There are 125 of them who report to work in Boeing Plant One each day with only one instruction: "Think". It doesn't matter *what* they think about as long as they do. I understand one man is wondering how he would plant a garden on the moon. Another wondered about making oxygen out of algae. Another has come up with an idea for making better use of wheat and another did something about a hydrofoil that probably will earn the Company quite a bit of money.)

Mr. Allen expressed the notion that people could think better in the Pacific Northwest than in some other parts of the world because of the climatic conditions . . . that the kind of mind that made it possible for Boeing to supply 40% of the air transportation of the Free World liked to relax with boats, skiing, fishing and other simple pursuits.

I then wondered aloud about something that every Seattleite has been wondering about for some years. "What was Mr. Allen's reaction the day that test pilot Tex Johnson did a slow roll over the Gold Cup race in the prototype of the 707?" For the benefit of those not acquainted with this interesting phenomenon, Johnson put an airplane with about a 135-foot wingspread through the approximate paces of a fighter plane over a crowd of about 500,000 people gathered on the shores of Lake Washington.

"Well," Allen said, with a smile mellowing his mental deliberations. "I was riding out to the races with Larry Bell, of Bell Aircraft. I had been kidding him some about the pills he kept taking for his heart condition.

"We had persuaded the Board of Directors to gamble $16-million dollars on that airplane. A number of our potential customers were on the ground watching it in the air over the race. When Tex did that slow roll, I recall having the presence of mind to say to Larry, 'Give me a couple of those pills!'"

When Mr. Johnson appeared before an extremely irate president of an extremely large corporation at 9 sharp the next morning, he was well aware of the possibility that he would be given an opportunity to re-try his skill as a riveter on the assembly line.

Exhibiting his training as an attorney, Allen said carefully, "Did anybody authorize you to do those slow rolls?"

Mr. Johnson said, "No, sir."

"Did something go wrong with the mechanism?"

"No, sir."

At this point, Mr. Allen ceased being a carefully calculating attorney and became the president of a very large corporation that could have gone broke if one of those wings had fallen off, not to mention the problems of the life of a test pilot he liked and those of a large portion of the population of the Pacific Northwest.

With unmistakable clarity, Mr. Allen said in loud tones, "Then why the ??!!!? hell did you do it!"

To me, the reply is the Boeing Company.

Tex Johnson said, "Mr. Allen, I had been flying that airplane. I knew what it could do. I knew it was the greatest piece of machinery that mankind has ever produced . . . and Mr. Allen, I had an audience of 500,000 people . . .

"Sir, I couldn't help it . . . I *couldn't* help it!"

As I was leaving to make room for a couple of generals, I like to think, I turned to Bill and said, "Is Boeing the largest manufacturer of aircraft in the world?"

He looked up at me with a twinkle in his eyes and said mildly, "Why yes, I believe it is."

* * *

Love's Labour Lost

Memo to matrimonially-minded maidens of college age: "This will come as a terrible surprise, but the University of Washington is not exclusively a state-supported husband hunting preserve."

A hundred years ago a San Francisco newspaper man noted that Seattle was a small town on the east side of Puget Sound about equidistant between Steilacoom and Port Townsend with little to recommend it but a University, which had a very fine building.

47

There have been occasions since when certain segments of our population, prodded by the poker of "advanced" thinking at the University ("advanced" but not necessarily correct), wish Daniel Bagley had been indicted and the whole thing had gone down the drain.

I am equally certain there have been times when some people at the University of Washington have wished the institution was located at a place some distance from that "stupid bunch of clowns that inhabit Seattle".

In between these divergent opinions is an interplay of the practical and the theoretical that has helped make both the city and the University great. Boeing, for example, needs basic knowledge supplied by the University and the University needs practical problems supplied by Boeing.

Although strongly resented in some quarters, our medical school has generally up-graded the practice of medicine and helped make Seattle a mecca for ailing bodies . . . and those bodies have provided practical problems for the medical school.

The same general theme applies to the schools of Fisheries, Law, Forestry, Architecture etc. And the picture is one of a University tugging away at a leash but only able to go as far as the community is willing. It wasn't willing, for example, to go for a medical school in 1892. Half-a-century later it was.

Undergraduates, of course, represent the bulk of the University's population. On the other hand, there are an estimated 5,000 persons on the campus engaged in research. With about $13-$14 million in research grants, we number among the top ten research universities in the country.

In addition to the information garnered directly by the research, that pool of 5,000 intellects, each with its own spirit of independence, is influencing its own little sphere.

Each time the city tries to settle back into an arm chair of stagnation, the University is the large tack that causes us to abruptly arise again.

And when the University gets too far out in "left" field, we jerk on the leash a little.

"*Century 21—We'll never make it*"

One of the traits of Seattleites is an atavistic compulsion toward negativism. I suppose that if we weren't allowed a reason for giving vent to it once in a while the entire population would end up psychotic.

And Century 21, like the A.Y.P. Exposition some 50 years ago, is giving us a grand excuse for an emotional binge. For example, we know that it is impossible to put 55,000 people per day through the turnstiles for a period of six months.

In 1909 we also "knew" they couldn't put 33,000 a day into an exposition at a location clear out at the end of the street car line—but they did. On their best day, they put 117,000 people through.

We know the management in charge of Century 21 is hopelessly inefficient—possibly even more so than the management at Boeing. It gives us pleasure to believe these things just as it gave us pleasure as children to occasionally rail against our parents. It gives us more than that—a sense of security —a somebody to be mad at that can't stop our paycheck.

I have a young son who usually says, "We'll never make it," as we're racing for the Fauntleroy ferry, not because he doesn't want to make it, but because he doesn't want an additional load of disappointment if we *really don't* make it.

But I think it is interesting to note that the men who are heading up Century 21 are successful in their own fields. We have obtained $15 million from the city, $10½ million from the state, and $9 million from the Federal government. We have a monorail that will pay for itself.

The cagey gentlemen at the top of Century 21 are not unlike our forefathers who considered a dollar an honest and wonderful thing to have. They're betting that we get enough people here to make the fair pay off and they've got more chips from various units of government than any fair this country ever had.

When it's over, we'll still have the Federal Science buildings, the Coliseum, Little Theater, a Fine Arts Pavilion, a concert-opera hall, and a spectacular Space Needle with a 60-foot jet of gas flame on top that will go into competition with Mt. Rainier as our major landmark.

So what?

Tourists and conventions are our third largest industry. We are in competition with Portland, San Francisco, Denver for convention business and we at present do not have a decent convention hall. After Century 21 we do.

Whether we like it or not, we need more people in this area to continue our growth as a major city. The A.Y.P. Exposition was the greatest shot in the arm we ever had outside of the Gold Rush and World War II.

I hate to disappoint the folks who think that nothing has happened in Seattle since the A.Y.P. Exposition in 1909. It opened on schedule, closed on schedule, made money . . .

But the creditors had the gates locked the day before it opened. They wanted their $40,000. Jacob Furth, the town's leading banker saved the day. He sent a letter to each of the 40 members of the board of trustees informing them they were to drop a check for $1,000 apiece in the mail that afternoon.

And as one of the trustees reminisces, "When Mr. Furth informed you you were to drop a check for $1,000 in the mail that afternoon, you dropped that check in the mail and didn't ask any questions."

* * *

University Properties . . . Another "heart" of the city

Another bit of internal pulling and hauling that helps us keep our civic muscles flexed is the matter of "pegging" the heart of the city. After looking at Cleveland, where I stayed at a motel in what might well have been the location of the major hotel . . or Los Angeles . . . cities where you're an hour or a $5 cab bill from the place where you're doing business, I'm glad that somebody strong and imaginative is in charge of the heart of our city.

I think, for example, that a tragic mistake has just been made in Portland with the upsurge of Lloyd's Center, across the river from the main part of town. Unlike our satellites, Northgate . . . Southgate . . . Bellevue . . . Lloyd's Center splits that city in half and makes doing business there more difficult.

When Denny Hill was taken down, a powerful effort was made to move the city to the regraded area.

50

I think we can thank University Properties (although I don't think we should overlook the Norton Building—and naturally the Central Association) for holding the line.

University Properties has a long-term lease on most of the property in downtown Seattle owned by the University of Washington. The other piece is the Olympic Hotel, but there is a complete unanimity of progressive management in both organizations.

When U.P. and Western Hotels came into the management of this tract in 1954, the picture was bleak. The former managers had reached all time high of $140,000 in annual payments to the University. I Magnin had moved from its former location at Fifth and Union. The buildings on the tract had been permitted to run down. Individual tenant leases all were at an end. An effort was being made to move the airline offices to the Denny Regrade. There were more real estate people than customers in the buildings trying to get them emptied.

And the U.P.-Western Hotels axis was signed to a lease that required annual payments of $3,000,000—not $140,000 —to the University.

I still remember the garbage cans lined up on the Fifth Avenue side of the Olympic Hotel. How would you like to try and sell quality merchandise across the street from a row of garbage cans?

Well, the folks who think that nothing has happened in Seattle since 1909 ought to take a look at this situation and

revise their thinking. We miss the old Metropolitan Theater, but the hotel's garbage cans are buried underneath the attractive new Plaza entrance to the hotel. Trees are blooming in their place.

The spectacular Washington Building has risen where the tiny, tired Douglas Building once was. University Properties blazed a new trail by swapping the U.S. Government a new post office for a piece of ground. And if you think it is easy to get the Federal government to do something that hasn't been done before at least 500 times, you have another guess coming.

Our Fifth Avenue now has the same quality connotation as the one in New York.

We're still weak in the block now occupied by the Olympic Hotel Garage, but don't think that University Properties is unaware of this. The next major building project will involve that property.

I think the Central Association helps to make the major difference in holding the line. Downtown businessmen comprise the Central Association. But there is a big difference over similar associations in other cities. Too often the practice has been to bring in outside planning groups to create a nicely-bound plan that just gathers dust.

Our program has been one of including businessmen . . . city and county elected officials in on the planning. As one gentleman said, "It ain't been easy," but everybody is aware of the problem of holding the heart of the city. There have been some bruised financial knuckles and noses in the process, but we are moving forward . . . we are holding the heart of our city intact.

Western Hotels . . . portrait of a present-day pioneer

Western Hotels is yet another reason why Seattle is the most important city in the Northwest 25% of the United States.

It is one of the nation's major hotel management chains; born in Seattle and now a vast network stretching half way around the world.

Seattle is building to a destiny linked with the Pacific rim. And like Boeing and Fisher Flouring Mills, Western Hotels is

52

pioneering the new frontier. They now have management of hotels in Guatemala, Mexico City, Los Angeles, San Francisco, Portland, Seattle, Vancouver and Anchorage. They are negotiating for facilities in Tokyo and Hong Kong and it wouldn't surprise me if they were taking a long look at India—the line of equal shipping costs between Seattle and New York.

Ours already is the third largest overseas airport in the United States. I am confident that one of these days our governmen will work out recognition of Red China. And Seattle is 360 miles closer to Tokyo than San Francisco.

Western Hotels is reaching out and establishing the kind of accommodations that wealthy Americans are accustomed to at home. They were in the forefront in the creation of Century 21. They have been a symbol of quality in the Pacific Northwest for half a century. Now they're reaching out for the whole world.

I once gave Western's president Eddie Carlson a quote from *Executive Suite* and the other day he tossed it back at me as expressing his philosophy. "The game's the thing. The money is just a system of keeping score."

I love the fact that this entire enterprise dates back to a day in 1903 when S. W. Thurston, founder of the chain, quit a touring tumbling act when it reached Seattle. Thurston was the top man on a human pyramid. The anchor man kept getting tipsy and Thurston had the longest distance to travel to the floor of the stage. He got his last "tumble" in Seattle . . . went out and got a job at a hotel . . . started Western Hotels.

* * *

"Frederick's" and the "Bon" . . . and the heart of Seattle

The fierce competition between our two major department stores, Frederick & Nelson and the Bon Marche, has shaped the face of our city, and helped preserve the city's heart.

Both stores once were located closer to Pioneer Square. Each store tried to acquire a whole city block that was not as far north as it now is. In each instance one or more property-owners "held out" a small piece of the block in hope of an exhorbitant profit. In each instance the holdouts "queered" the deal and forced the stores to their present locations on Pine Street. And the property that might have been used is not

53

as valuable as that occupied by the stores or the satellite stores around them.

"Frederick's" (never referred to by any other name), is a reflection of Seattle's personality "as we would like to be". When the surviving partner, D. E. Frederick, decided to retire, he looked over the United States for the firm he felt would most likely continue the Frederick's tradition . . . picked Marshall Field and effected the sale. I understand this was a new concept with Marshall Field and the start of their expansion beyond Chicago.

I think it is of interest that two thousand women pay $2 apiece each year for the privilege of attending an "Import" fashion tea. As a result, the style-conscious women of our city are more knowledgeable about clothes than even their counterparts on Fifth Avenue in New York City.

The "Bon" is an Allied Stores' outlet that has moved into the mercantile field with the slogan "we will not be undersold by anybody." For a long time, under local management, the Bon was the secondary department store. Under present management it is very much a competitor of Frederick's.

Although there is mutual respect, there still are fundamental differences of management opinion. The Bon turned to Monday night opening immediately. Frederick's didn't succumb for 3 years because the management felt Seattle people really preferred to be at home at night. The Bon serves cocktails. Frederick's does not.

I'm not going to get in the middle on which store sells the most merchandise, but between them their sales are about $70 million a year.

Individually, neither store sells as much as the major and dominant department store in Portland. Their combined volume is about 35% more. But that doesn't begin to tell the whole story. Nobody in Seattle has a "corner" on the merchandise market.

We have vigorously healthy satellite stores like Best's and Magnin's . . . Littler's . . . John Doyle Bishop . . . Albert's . . . and Nordstrom's, the biggest independent shoe store in the world . . . the best Penney's store in the U.S.

54

Both stores have suburban shopping centers. But that's what the latter are, "suburban". Thanks to Frederick's and the Bon there are better prices in Seattle—within walking distances—than in most cities.

Seattle is the mecca for major shopping expeditions from as far north as Alaska . . . east to at least Spokane, and easily south to Portland.

* * *

Even Clubs . . . now and then

The spirit of competition in Seattle's economic community is so lively that we even resort to something so primitive as "Clubs".

Without hesitation, I would estimate that 50% of the business in Seattle is transacted over the luncheon tables of the Rainier Club, the Washington Athletic Club and the Harbor Club. At one time, this figure was nearer 100%, but the advent of our plush restaurants has cut into this territory savagely in the past decade.

The Rainier Club, established before 1900 by the top men in our business community was the number one "status symbol" for so many years that pro-communist publications were not one whit diverted from attacking it by the advent of the immensely popular Washington Athletic Club in 1931.

More recently the Harbor Club, with an unsurpassed view of the city's transportation sinews and backed by the same business echelon as the Rainier Club, has had the temerity to challenge the latter's venerable position.

PART II

in which we consider
methods of taking
advantage of seattle.

SEE THE SIGHTS... A FRIENDLY LITTLE TOUR CO

About "Faces"

Any city has about it certain areas and landmarks that give it character and individuality. I think, for instance, of Fifth Avenue and the Bowery in New York . . . Union Square and the Mission District in my other favorite city, San Francisco.

I think our important ones are Pioneer Square . . . Salt Water Strip (Yesler-University) . . . Pike Place Market . . . Fifth Avenue Axis (University-Pine) . . . Broadway East (Pine-Roy).

Being younger and on the move, Seattle is in a greater state of flux than many of our cities. For example, we have gained about 100,000 in population in each of the last two decades while population has decreased in both New York and San Francisco.

We recently obtained natural gas, which means the ultimate elimination of the gas plant on Lake Union . . . a huge freeway is in the process of bisecting our city. It may be covered and create a "central park" or uncovered and cut the city in half. A second bridge is being built across Lake Washington. Our patterns of business and entertainment are continuously changing . . . and should national foreign policy permit it we may participate in the explosive economic changes in Asia.

This section shows Seattle as we see it at this moment. (summer, 1961). Our weekly publication, *The Seattle Guide*, has depicted the changing Seattle scene for 38 years and will continue to do so on a current weekly basis.

And now, "About Faces" . . .

* * *

Pioneer Square, 1961—the rebirth of the "skidroad" . . .

Over half-a-century ago a logger in from one of the camps to celebrate Saturday night observed the crowd of merrymakers jamming Pioneer Square and is alleged to have said, "By golly, this looks like the skidroad!"

The skidroad of those days was a logging road leading into the forests. Small round trees were imbedded in the road at right angles every six or eight feet and the huge logs that built our economy were "skidded" down to tidewater. These roads were jammed with men and animals during the working day.

The word "skidroad" has been aborted to "skid row" in some quarters—probably because some writer didn't listen carefully when he was taking his notes and inadvertently did the wrong translation during an interview. The connotation has come to be one of a rundown part of any city.

Ours is being reborn—not with loggers and horses, but with young men in oxford gray suits and ladies with mink stoles attending jazz sessions lubricated by beer and a Gay Nineties atmosphere. (There is even a $6 ice cream sundae called the "Pioneer Square" available).

And the place reeks with tradition.

There is supposed to be a bronze plaque on the Mutual Life Building commemorating the fact that our first industry, Henry Yesler's mill, was located there but I couldn't find it. In 1869, for example, Yesler borrowed $45,000 to rebuild his mill after a fire. When he repaid the loan 12 years later it cost him $146,000—*a hundred-and-one-thousand-dollars in interest, or 19% per year!*

It is said that in the panic of 1895, the location of every single $20-goldpiece in the city was known to the entire business community. Within the next decade about $250,000,000 passed through the vaults of Pioneer Square banks. Some of the vaults can be seen today in "Elroy's" a late-night snack-and-ice cream parlor. (You actually eat at a table in one of the vaults.)

60

Within a year of the discovery of gold in 1897, some 8,000 miners had been "outfitted" here on the way north. We outmaneuvered other Pacific Northwest cities and got the government assay office located in Pioneer Square so the raw gold was converted to money here. We caught them coming and going. No wonder we became the youngest big city in the United States. (194% pop. increase, 1900-1910).

Non Bastardi Carborundum . . .

Jack London, San Francisco's prized "relic", had his origin here—the illegitimate son of Henry Yesler's maid and a traveling astrologist. Forty thousand tons of San Francisco's Nob Hill lies underneath the buildings here. It was brought up as ballast in the ships that returned with pilings for San Francisco's piers.

When it was new, the Pioneer Building was cited in architectural magazines as one of the most beautiful in the nation. Not cited was a "bridge of sighs" constructed from this center of business activity across the alley some six stories up so our businessmen could visit their "girl friends" in the Butler Hotel without the risk of encountering their wives.

Before the "big" Seattle fire, the street was one story lower than it is today and the original store fronts can be found in the basements of some of the buildings.

The present totem pole, patterned after the original one which our businessmen stole from Alaska some 60 years ago, was carved in Alaska as part of a W.P.A. project in 1939.

The most expensive meal in Seattle's history was bought here. A gentleman who slipped away from the jury on which he was serving was fined $300 for "eating out" . . . The town's leading gambler shot and killed the chief of police a block away and was released by a jury which stated that after all, "the chief shot first" . . . Three men were lynched just off Pioneer Square on James Street. A grand jury held the lynching was justified and saved the state a lot of money in prosecution costs. An historian reported the lynchings had an extremely salutary effect on our lawless element for several months.

Geographically, it is the narrowest part of Seattle's Waist. It's one of the crossroads for our north and south bound buses. And industry seeking convenient bus travel for its employees is

61

beginning to re-locate here and participate in the rejuvenation of the heart of our city.

* * *

Fishermen's Terminal . . . Locks and Lox

Principal commercial use of the Government Locks, is to bring our fishing fleet, the largest in the nation, to its berth in Salmon Bay.

A terminal that enables a thousand fishing boats to tie up at one time . . . boats ranging from 18 to 100 feet in length and from 100 to 1,000 miles of seascape in search of one of the world's most nutritious foods. It has ten times as many fishing boats as those at San Francisco's "Fishermen's Wharf". And they bring in the biggest crop of salmon and halibut in the world.

Predominantly Scandinavian, this fleet is our 3rd or 4th largest industry, accounting for about $50 million income a year to the city. A real, working terminal with broad open spaces and fishermen repairing their nets and boats during respites from one of the world's most speculative and dangerous occupations . . . a challenge that attracts the strong individualists who make up a strong portion of our population.

I love the fact that the "Halibut Fishermen's Wives" is one of the organizations that appears frequently on the society pages of our daily newspapers . . . and that twin cartoons appear on the walls of a ship chandlery here: One depicts two fishermen in a tavern with two girls. The balloons above the men's heads reveal they are talking about nothing but fishing. The other shows the same men at sea fishing. And the balloons above their heads? They're talking about the two gals in the tavern.

Lox? Kosher-smoked salmon that puts New York's Atlantic version to shame for delicacy of flavor even if it isn't as red.

* * *

The Arboretum—"we can grow darn near anything . . ."

The dictionary defines an Arboretum as a place where trees and shrubs are cultivated for scientific or educational purposes. This doesn't begin to state what our Arboretum means to the people of Seattle.

It's as much a part of our personality as the clean clear air after a rain. One diminutive old lady reports to the Arboretum office once each week to find out which part of "her" garden she should weed. Every year, on "work-and-fun-day", a thousand women report for gardening duty.

Unlike our parks, this is a "working" botannical garden. Because of our mild climate, we can grow almost anything. And because of its location only a few blocks from the population center of Metropolitan Seattle, it is easily accessible to all.

It is not unusual for 10,000 people to enjoy "their" garden on a single day. Recently a Japanese tea garden, probably the most perfect outside of Japan, has become the focal point of this unique feature of our personality. The teahouse was given us by the city of Tokyo. Key stones were crated and sent here from Japan. The garden was designed by a top Japanese landscape architect who supervised the exact placement of each rock and tree, wearing a beret, cigarette holder and a pair of immaculate tennis shoes—in spite of the mud.

Public revulsion reached one of its hottest pitches when some unthinking and drinking University students vandalised the teahouse. The judgement against them was never again, for the rest of their lives, could they enter the Arboretum— *and they don't!*

The Arboretum, all 260 acres—is a part of us . . . and we are a part of it.

* * *

The Government Locks—second largest on this continent?

Although congress informed us in 1956 that henceforth we were to call these the "Hiram Chittenden" locks after an engineer who was rather important in their construction, they will never be anything other than the "Government" locks . . . any more than the new "Seattle Center" will be anything other than the Civic Center.

These locks were constructed at the same general time the government was building another set in the Panama Canal Zone and we have always "known" they were second in size only to those. The fact that this is not true does not matter. As far as we're concerned they're the second largest locks on the continent.

This is a very good thing from a promotional standpoint because as many people "visit" the locks each year (1,500,000)

63

as visit Mt. Rainier. About 80,000 boats per year go through the locks. A tremendous percentage of those are pleasure boats.

The locks, of course, weren't constructed for the benefit of pleasure boats. The theory was that the shipping of the world would beat a pathway to Lakes Union and Washington to drop their barnacles and tie up at tideless, teredo-less piers.

This hasn't happened, thank heaven, or our lakes would be totally commercial. On the other hand, it has helped us build the greatest commercial fishing fleet in the world . . . a fleet which can take advantage of the fresh-water situation. And it really doesn't matter what kind of boats are going through the locks. The business of lowering them as much as 22 feet is a fascinating thing to peoples from Iowa—or Seattle.

* * *

"Pike Place—what do you know, a 'farmer's market' with farmers!"

Like most other parts of the country, we are faced with the inevitable fact that a ball park . . . housing developments . . . the Boeing Company have usurped land that once was used by truck gardeners . . . that it's a heck of a lot harder to raise a carrot than to operate a lift truck, and possibly for less money . . . that the neighborhood supermarkets have moved into the "market" business on a major scale.

I suppose these are "improvements" like the replacement of our cable cars with buses. On the other hand, if you have visited the "market places" of the rest of the world, or if you remember the way things used to be—or if you have visited the Pike Place Market in recent months—you will understand the soul-satisfying pleasure of buying your vegetables from the man who brought them into existence for you.

In addition to the fact that he is one of the last surviving "individualists" in our world, he usually provides you with a better price than even the big chains. And he is a pleasure to encounter . . . a refreshing experience. I think his tomatoes are redder, his celery crisper, his lettuce fresher than those which can be found anyplace else.

With all due respect, the chain store offers you 30 or 40 feet of "produce". The Pike Place Market offers you a full city block of competing individuals who usually give you a better price. They also offer you an exciting, elbow-rubbing experience.

Nobody is paying me for this "plug", but I am pledging that I, myself, will buy at the Pike Place Market at least once a week because I think it is one of the most colorful places Seattle has to offer and because there are "bargains" here and because it helps preserve a tradition of individuality.

I doubt if there is another "market" in the country that has 70—count 'em, 70—individual farmers offering the best they can raise in our land for your consideration.

The "Return of the Native" (I'm referring to you) will continue it as one of our most famous landmarks.

* * *

The Floating Bridge on Lake Washington

Along with Mt. Rainier and the up-coming "Space Needle", we consider this one of our most important accomplishments. There is little doubt it provides one of the most beautiful entrances to any city in the United States—if you don't happen to catch it during peak traffic hours when it can be somewhat frustrating.

Of course, there was the usual virulent opposition to it when it was first proposed, a natural reaction to anything new in Seattle. There was considerable difficulty persuading the insurance companies to insure it, although there was no problem getting insurance on the Tacoma Narrows bridge which blew down.

* * *

Our folksy ferry system—the largest in the world . . .

Ever since one unfortunate soul drove on one of our ferries and then proceeded to drive through it and off of the other end, there has been a speed limit on the Washington State ferry system. They feel very kindly toward their commuters and try to take care of them.

The chains at the ends of the ferries have been strengthened and the deckhands caution against excessive speed even though they don't issue speeding tickets. The personnel fail to recognize that Boeing workers keep decks of cards hidden under the seats for a little poker coming and going from their shifts. They recognize that people like me, on the last trip, are in danger of missing our destination because we're asleep. The banging on car doors is strictly routine as they startle the folks awake.

When the state took over the system a few years back, they attempted to institute a "toot-toot" on arriving at a dock. Traditionally, there had been a "toooot-toot-toot" and the uproar from the populace over the change was such that you get the traditional "toooot-toot-toot" upon your arrival.

The system started with 3 ferries in 1919, from Seattle to West Seattle, Des Moines to Maury Island and Tacoma to Gig Harbor. The first Bremerton ferry, the *Bailey Gatzert,* started in 1920. In 1935 we bought and remodelled our most publicized ferry, the *Kalakala.* The system carries eight million passengers a year . . . 2,600,000 cars.

They "could" charge you if your car stalls and you have to make an extra trip, but they usually don't have the heart for it. For some reason, children are compelled to "run" on the deck. For you and for me, the system provides spectacular views of the Sound and city . . . of the San Juan Islands.

66

For the kids, it is an interesting new place to have something to eat—and what is more important, a new and interesting place to go to the bathroom.

* * *

"We hope to make our University an educational institution the football team will be proud of" —Provost Fred Thieme at the showing of the first Rose Bowl championship films.

It's kind of a dirty trick to use the above quote unless the total picture is explained. It was made at a time when football enthusiasm was running pretty high and Fred was making the point that there were other facets to the University.

The more serious purpose of the University previously has been touched on in this book. But the physical plant is one of the most beautiful in the world. It is on a slope north of the ship canal and faces Mt. Rainier according to a plan originally put together for the Alaska-Yukon-Pacific Exposition in 1909.

It comprises 605 acres of wide rolling lawns, formal beds of flowers and shrubs and a variety of native trees surrounding buildings in a generally-Gothic style. However, one male observer pointed out the beauty was not confined to the buildings and grounds. "You should see the beauty to behold on a windy spring day when the coeds are climbing the steps of Denny Hall between classes," he said.

The University once stood where the Olympic Hotel now is. We owe the present campus to the AYP Exposition, which was successful thanks to the best-kept secret Seattle ever had. Shortly before the Exposition there was an outbreak of bubonic plague in the city. About a dozen people had it . . . thousands of rats were afflicted. The rats were centered around the city's outhouses.

In the biggest "back fence" whispering campaign in history the health authorities spread the word to "get rid of the rats". For a period of weeks, I am told, nobody entered a privy without carrying a gun.

The "Gold Cup Race"—the world's biggest spectator sport

A decade ago we had never heard of unlimited hydroplane racing. Then a Seattle-built boat, the Slo-Mo, won the top trophy in that field and the citizenry went wild over the mighty roar, the danger and the hot competition among the world's fastest boats.

It's certainly the most thrilling, best-attended (200,000 to 500,000 spectators) collection of mayhem since they put a ban on feeding Christians to the lions. People camp overnight on the shores of Lake Washington to get good observation points. Downtown Seattle is empty and parking is jammed for miles around the lake during these midsummer races. The litter left behind adds up to more tons than Nero's Park Department (not ours) could cope with.

We had the Gold Cup . . . lost it and staged the *Seafair Trophy Race* in its stead . . . and then regained it. But the race, by any other name, will still be the Gold Cup to Seattleites.

The Smith Tower . . . (Note): Publication of information about this city without mentioning this building is not permitted.

This building is 42 stories high and from the top people who will ride the elevators at a cost of 50c have a spectacular view.

It was "bulled" through by the son of the L. C. Smith typewriter man as a means of "pegging" the town around it because he had bought up a substantial amount of property here.

He was considered an unmitigated idiot by some people, because the city moved north. But maybe his judgement wasn't so bad after all. There are labor pains that look like a re-birth down below in Pioneer Square.

The Norton Building—Air Apparent . . .

In our opinion this is the most spectacular new building in Seattle, and this is an important statement when you consider the new Logan Building . . . Washington Building . . . Library . . . and addition to City Light.

It also is the city's most expensive building, $12,000,000. Washington Building is next at $10,000,000. It's all windows and reflective so you have the feeling of fresh air rather than a building. It is an important building to the city in that it was built in the financial district at a time when the city was rapidly growing north and leaving the lower end of the city behind. This has helped to peg the heart of our city.

Operated by some of our most forward-looking citizens, it contains, for example, the Harbor Club which is challenging the venerable Rainier Club in prestige of membership. It has a spectacular view of the harbor and our industrial section. It's an almost totally automatic building that can be operated by only two people—an elevator starter and an engineer.

* * *

The New City Hall. Oh dear, they argued for months over whether Fifth Avenue would cave in during construction . . . and sure enough, they were right. It did. Detour.

They considered having a competition to name the new building, but our forthright mayor said, "Let us not waste the

69

money. No matter what we name it, the folks will call it the City Hall."

It's like the Aurora Bridge. Nobody knows its real name is the "George Washington Memorial Bridge" . . . or cares.

The Association of Sidewalk Superintendents, which supervised the "observation" platform across the street, has a by-law prohibiting constructive suggestions . . . only criticism.

* * *

Seattle Art Museum . . . our cultural fountainhead

People of the Pacific Northwest adorn the walls of their homes with the "work" of local artists to a greater extent and with more discernment than in any other part of the country.

We have some of the world's finest artists in Mark Tobey . . . Kenneth Callahan . . . Morris Graves.

Not all of this, of course, is attributable to the Seattle Art Museum. On the other hand, it was a major cultural "break through" nearly thirty years ago when the city council authorized Dr. Richard Fuller and his mother to erect one of the finest art museums in the country in the proper setting of Volunteer Park. It was a sign of our emerging cultural maturity.

Some indication of the meaning of the museum to Seattle people came with a travelling Japanese art collection a few years back. Attendance at the collection was "clocked"—for reasons I don't know about—in Boston, Chicago and Seattle. One in 82 Boston people attended . . . one in 67 in Chicago . . . one in 7 in Seattle.

There are a lot of explanations for these figures, the most likely being that we "outpublicized" the exhibit when it was here. But the fact is we "use" our art museums and we have learned to appreciate art to the extent that we buy the works of Northwest artists for our homes and are aware of what that art is saying.

Although it was in part because of financial feasibility, the fact is that we have in this museum a world famous Oriental art collection. I think of this particularly because some years ago, in the jade collection, a friend of mine found the "Great Seal of China" here . . . a huge piece of jade used for centuries to make documents official in that country. It made news all

70

over the world because the "seal" had been missing for decades . . .

One of Seattle's most beautiful "faces" . . .

* * *

"The Seattle Center? Yeah, that's where they had 'the Fair'."—Any Seattleite after 1962.

As this is being written, the entire population around here is being swept into the vortex of a major World's Fair called Century 21 . . . an exciting and disrupting event from which our city will emerge with convention facilities that only five other U.S. cities can begin to match.

It is another step by which Seattle seeks to maintain its supremacy as the major city in the Northwest 25% of the United States. Our first "Fair", the A.Y.P. Exposition in 1909 was a part of our city's most explosive growth—the 1900-1910 decade when the population increase was 194%. The second greatest increase came as a result of World War II when we went from the 22nd largest city in the country to the 19th largest.

The percentage of increase was smaller (27%) in the 1940-50 decade, but the actual count was only 50,000 less. And in the earlier period the city more than doubled its size through annexations. In the latter case thousands of troops went overseas through our port, liked the city they saw . . . returned to make it their home.

Good, big conventions do the same thing for a city. They bring in people. They bring in new industries. As one of nine "amenity" regions in the U.S. it is important to our solid growth that key people are exposed to the pleasure of living in our mild, stimulating climate. We are in competition with Portland, Denver, San Francisco for convention business.

The new center helps make us a tough competitor. It gives us a modern, covered Coliseum providing *four acres* of unobstructed space—not a pillar . . . big enough to house a national political convention . . . 129,000 feet of exhibit space . . . a basketball court with room for 18,000 spectators. The only other cities in the whole country who have these are New York, Philadelphia, Chicago, Los Angeles and San Francisco.

And, outside of San Francisco, I can't imagine anyone who

71

would want to attend a mid-summer convention voluntarily in any of the other cities.

In addition to the Coliseum, the residium of the Fair will include a spacearium provided by the Boeing Company which will take people off into "space" until actually going off into space becomes old hat . . . a "Sunflower Fountain" with lights and music, covering half-a-city block with a 60-nozzle display . . . A science pavilion . . . 3,100-seat opera house . . . 800-seat little theater . . . an arena seating 5,500 . . . a non-figurative mural 60 by 17 feet . . . a Plaza of States featuring a capsule description of each United State, and—

A Space Needle that will rise about 750 feet above sea-level with a 60-foot gas flame on top . . . a spectacular piece of engineering ingenuity that will put ordinary people higher than they have ever been in this city . . . a landmark rival to Mt. Rainier . . . the Eiffel Tower of Seattle—with the addition of a fine restaurant making slow revolutions to provide diners with the greatest view of an area that has some of the most breath-taking scenery in the world.

* * *

"Seattle seems unanimously in favor of removing the balance of this mountain and casting it into the sea."—Harvard Business Review, July, 1930

In 1851, David Denny, who was in charge of constructing the city's first building—a log cabin at Alki Point—wrote his brother, "Come as soon as you can. We have found a valley that will support a thousand families."

He probably was referring to the Duwamish Valley, which was inhabited by a river generally meandering like a huge snake around the territory now occupied by Boeing Field . . . the Boeing Company and Harbor Island.

It is certain he wasn't thinking of the present location of the city center, which was a steep, heavily-forested hillside broken up by deep ravines. Topographically, it was a most unlikely spot for a city.

At that time the outlet to Lake Washington was through the lowlands around Renton and into the Duwamish River.

The lake was 9 feet higher than it is today. Seward Park was an island.

The gently-sloping area east of our depots along Jackson Street was a hill as high as a ten-story building. The top of the New Washington Hotel approximates the top of what once was Denny Hill. Everything south of the King Street Station once was tidelands.

We were obsessed by the necessity of washing down our hills and filling in our hollows and in the process changed the location of about 45,000,000 cubic yards of dirt, enough to build a dirt road to New York with a return by a different route.

Evidence of our changed contours still exist. Look down at First and Seneca. This once was a 75-foot deep ravine. Frederick & Nelson's location once was a bog. The bridge over Dearborn Street is over a "cut". Third, Fourth and Fifth Avenues south of the Olympic Hotel once were from 15 to 26 feet higher. Harbor Island, dredged from the sea, was the biggest man-made island in the world until the advent of Treasure Island in San Francisco.

* * *

Museum of History and Industry—our status symbol . . .

I have a strong feeling that "dust" is not permitted in this attractive and totally modern structure . . . not on the exhibits and not on the thinking that lies behind this portrayal of Seattle as it once was and now is.

It seems to me that too often the connotation of a museum is summed up in the word "stuffy" . . . and an historical museum is something controlled by a small clique preserving the past as it reflects their own families.

Our museum has reached one plateau—for a young city. We recognize that we have a past. We also recognize we have a present . . . and possibly even a future. The museum is a dynamic institution with a constantly changing program against a basic background of our history.

It is an integral part of our community, from the men who give tremendous sums to make the various major sections possible to the Girl Scouts cleaning huge Indian baskets and sing-

ing "rock 'n roll". The aviation wing has the Boeing B-1, for example. (We all know about the B-29 and the 707. Few of us know the B-1 was the first contract mail plane. Made of wood, wire and cloth, it logged 350,000 miles between here and Victoria, Vancouver.) There's a $150,000 Maritime Wing and an upcoming Natural History Wing costing $160,000.

It is a constantly-changing and constantly intriguing "show" featuring everything from Leonardo Da Vinci inventions to the cavalcade of aviation.

Operated almost entirely by volunteers, it has about 200,-000 "volunteer" visitors each year . . . people who are proving that maybe it's true the best things in life are free.

* * *

"Port of Seattle—What Port?" Joseph W. Doaks

To the average citizen, Seattle is a seaport city with a lot of water in its front yard but no ships. He whisks along the Alaskan Way Viaduct at 45 miles an hour, notes no ships tied up at the piers below and leaps to this conclusion.

He is totally unaware the piers he sees are too short for big ships. They can't be lengthened because the water is too deep. But they can and will be used with spectacular success as motels and restaurants and shops.

The shipping has moved to the East and West Waterways on either side of our man-made Harbor Island where it is tucked out of sight of the average Joe Doaks. He would be utterly astonished to learn the port generates $340 million worth of business a year . . . is our second largest industry . . . provides direct employment for 16,000 people . . . that our airport, operated by the Port of Seattle, has the third largest overseas traffic in the United States.

It's sort of a comforting thought that every time you see an ocean-going freighter chugging down a channel it's worth about $50,000 to our economy.

We love canals around here and there presently is agitation for one between Seattle and Tacoma, which may seem ridiculous on the face, but would provide sea-level factory sites currently considered indispensable for world trade competition.

An interesting thought is held by most of our businessmen. It goes like this: "If somehow we could work out recognition of Red China it would mean our waterfront would operate at a war-time peak—permanently."

* * *

Our sweet success—or down by the sewer side

Thousands of people drive through the University of Washington Arboretum every day. And those with a more artistic sensitivity often admire the lovely arches of the aquaduct that crosses overhead near the north entrance. Artists admire its graceful lines; a watercolor of it hangs in the Arboretum clubhouse.

Almost no one wonders why it's there. And among even those I've found, none realizes it's one of our main trunk sewers. It connects with a siphon under the ship canal where it enters the main north trunk sewer, proceeds along the north side of the canal until it is siphoned back and runs under Fort Lawton and empties into Puget Sound.

Ordinarily, the matter of sewers is not a subject of polite dinner table conversation, but we're recognized as the city with the most publicized sewers in America. Not long ago, that north

75

trunk sewer went berserk, sucked a hole a city block square into its depths before the problem was corrected.

Our sewers take care of some 32 inches of rain which the Lord provides each year to help us keep our streets clean. In addition, the City Engineer's office flushes our streets with 100,000,000 gallons of water a year. This is enough water to fill Green Lake to a depth half-a-foot higher than it now is. Thanks to our hills and sewers, the runoff is no problem. (And as an added fillip, our engineers sweep up a mound of dirt 70 feet high and 200 feet in diameter every year).

At the moment we're sitting on a thousand miles of sewers and within a few years that length will seem infinitesimal. The original system cost about $26-million. As a result of a major sewer publicity effort we voted in a Metropolitan Sewer System that will circle Lake Washington at a cost of $135 million . . . probably the largest developed from a single plan and built in one program in the country.

* * *

We proudly present . . . our 'showcase' of information

Although the average person probably doesn't understand why, I think it is significant that since it recently emerged as one of our most open and beautiful buildings, the use of the main branch of the Seattle Public Library has increased forty per cent.

Nobody lucky enough to visit Seattle should leave without seeing the outdoor fountain of George Tsutakawa, which recently was featured on the cover of "Interbuild", an English architectural magazine. It probably is the most frequently photographed object in the city.

The Library has taken a tip from our modern department stores in making the stock pleasantly available for the customers—and has added comfortable lounges and tables.

A group of experts recently made the statement that no growing, vigorous city could meet its destiny without the presence of a readily available library with a vast font of pertinent information for progress.

With our new library, coordinated to beauty and utility

76

from the outside to the "stacks", we not only meet that need but provide an "open" space that helps us preserve the heart of our city.

At least half of our adult population uses it. The books that are loaned every day the library is open would make a pile at least 2½ times the height of the Smith Tower—which is a lot of books to put back on the shelves.

And if by any chance you care, the more interesting information contained in the compilation of this volume came from books, manuscripts, and microfilms provided by this facility.

* * *

"THE MIGHTY MOUNTAIN . . ."

Mt. Rainier is not a recognized formal religion in the state of Washington as it once was among the Indians. Yet it exercises a profound influence on our spiritual lives.

We call it *The Mountain*, for instance. It is always different . . . always dominating . . . always spectacular. It compels us to lift our eyes from our routine for a quick flash of inspiration that is above and beyond our daily strivings.

It's the symbol of natural beauty that makes us want to live here. Yet it's a reminder that we're here only on a temporary basis. It has claimed the lives of 80 people since the first fatal fall in 1897. Thirty two of these were in a military plane that crashed on The Mountain in 1946. Ten years earlier 23-year-old Delmar Fadden succumbed to an irresistible urge to make the first winter ascent to the top. He made it. We know that because we found a willow branch he had planted on Columbia Peak. The rangers found his body halfway down the mountain the next spring.

Mt. Rainier got its start as a part of an uplift 12 million years ago that created the Cascade Range. About 2 million years ago it became a part of the *Pacific Circle of Fire* which includes such volcanoes as Fujii, Krakatau, Erebus, Popocatepetl. Through a series of eruptions, it built itself from 6,000 to

16,000 feet. Not more than several thousand years ago, it blew off the top 2,000 feet.

The last recorded eruptions of smoke and dust were in 1870. But we know that Fuji, a sister volcano, remained dormant for 1,000 years before exploding again. Another sister, Paricutan, came into existence in a Mexican corn field in 1943. Rainier's 26 volcanoes, which had been receding for centuries, started growing again in 1945.

The Mountain unquestionably is the number one attraction for out-of-state visitors. But a prime indication of its impact on us is that of the 1,500,000 visitors last year, three quarters of them were people who came from within the boundaries of the state.

* * *

SHOPPING

Priceless Prowling—a conscientious compilation of interesting and unusual shopping opportunities in Seattle . . .

There's a story about a Seattle woman who went to New York for a shopping "binge" and returned without buying anything because "there was so much to buy I just got confused."

Why?

Specifically, retail merchandising in Seattle has reached

a well-balanced and highly-competitive situation. We have been able to attract talented buyers who exercise excellent judgment in the buying marts of the world. We have created extremely pleasant "atmospheres" in our shops.

This has resulted in a great freedom of choice for the shopper and a competitive price structure.

The net result is an enormous influx of shoppers from Alaska, Canada, eastern Washington and Oregon.

The following does not purport to be all-inclusive. It does include an interesting variety of the outstanding, unusual —or both.

DEPARTMENT STORES

Frederick & Nelson, Fifth & Pine—Considered by many the most beautiful department store in the world . . . one of few U.S. stores which maintains permanent buying offices in Europe. Noteworthy departments:

Steuben Shop—Only one in Pacific Northwest.
Gun Shop—Has one of top U.S. gun experts.
Seattle Shop—Carefully selected gifts with NW accent.
Elizabeth Arden Salon—part of complete beauty salon.
Kindergarten — Well equipped & supervised. Free to shoppers.

The Bon Marche, Fourth & Pine—Largest in the Northwest . . . known as the "drive in department store" since advent of sky bridge for pedestrians from garage across the street . . . they aggressively state, "We are *never* undersold!" Noteworthy departments:

Budget Floor—bargains . . . biggest in Western U.S.
High School & College Shops—big play for young fashions.
Home Furnishings—3 floors, each 1 block square.
Yardage Shop—sold as "Fashion Fabrics".
Fashion Circle—Women's departments in capsule form.

CLOTHING STORES—WOMEN

Best's Apparel, Fifth & Pine—"For young women of all ages" atmosphere of being modern and spritely . . . quick with newest fashions and on to the newer . . . not connected with New York's.

I. Magnin's, Sixth & Pine—A jewel box of a store . . . reputation for style and quality that causes women to carefully hang their coats over the chair so the IMCO label shows . . . Laykins, internationally-known jewelry shop, is here . . . discriminating men's department.

John Doyle Bishop, Fifth & Union—Small, fine, selective . . . in excellent taste . . . on Fifth Avenue lane of fine shops.

CLOTHING STORES—MEN

Albert's Ltd., 5th near University—Delightful, understated Old English decor . . . such relaxed and casual atmosphere it's hard to realize the well-dressed salesmen aren't just around to make you feel at home.

Littler's, Union & 5th, and Olympic Hotel—If men hung their coats over chairs in public, Littler's is the label they'd make sure showed . . . it appeals to the man interested in style . . . has a very good women's shop on corner . . . especially good in spectator sports.

CLOTHING STORES—CHILDREN

Fairy Frocks, Broadway E. & Roy—Founded 30 years ago on fine custom-made clothes . . . noted as one of the best on the coast . . . girls, infancy to 15 years . . . boys, to 7 years. (Just now expanded to women's clothes).

McCann's, 6th near Olive—Only downtown shop devoted to boys' and young men's clothing . . . long established leader.

Merry Go Round, 5th & University—Bountiful supply of clothes and toys for young people of both sexes . . . displayed tantalizingly for doting parents and grandparents.

Pied Piper, E. Madison near 41st—This is like "bringing out our own private stock" . . . in our neighborhood . . . exceptional in its selections . . . little sister to the *Assembly Room* (in next block) which carries fine sports clothes for women.

SHOE STORES

Nordstrom's, 5th & Pike—One of the largest shoe stores in the world . . . and to us one of the finest . . . shoes for everyone plus a shoe rack in the basement where you help yourself to bargains.

Frank Moore, 5th near Pine—New and elegant women's shoe store . . . plush and brocade . . . with shoes displayed on beautiful antiques.

FURNITURE—ACCESSORIES

Wm. L. Davis, 5th & University—First store in NW exclusively devoted to fine furniture and design . . . founded in 1890—generally traditional styles . . . Antique Galleries (north end of the block) carries beautiful European and Oriental antiques.

Del Teet, Broadway E. near Olive—Leaders in contemporary furnishings . . . have designed and furnished some of the more outstanding NW interiors . . . are attracting other good furniture and decor shops into a Broadway E. nucleus, i.e. *Robert McBreen, R. J. Skewes.*

B. K. Alsin, Union & 6th—Importers of interior furniture, et al. . . . generally Danish . . . small and very tasty.

Keegs, Olive near Broadway E.—Pioneered the tasteful accessory habit in Seattle . . . also interior design and Danish furniture now . . . best browsing in town.

Miller-Pollard, University Way near E. 45th—Another shop with contemporary merchandise by talented buyers . . . often have exhibits of NW craftsmen . . . noted color analysts . . . full of ideas for you when you're temporarily at a loss for one.

Wallpapers, Inc. 1705 Olive Way—Miles and miles of wallpaper . . . wall height panels for mental viewing on that wall at home . . . located in Decorative Center of related businesses.

NATIONALITY SHOPS

Finlandia Arts, Seneca near 6th—Small shop of large selection of Arabia dinnerware . . . (don't be confused by the name—made in Helsinki) . . . Swedish, Finnish, Danish crystal and stainless steel.

Haru's, Pine near Broadway E.—The best of Oriental originality displayed in contemporary accessories and furniture . . . look for the Soma cups, double layered for insulation . . . or the iron teapots that make the most flavorful tea and don't drip.

Philippine Shop, University Way near 42nd—The handicrafts

of the Philippines . . . wood carving, embroidering, hand-loomed items . . . hemp and raffia uses in the modern home.

Kawabe, 4th Ave. in Olympic Hotel—Good selection of Japanese wares and clothing . . . in central shopping district.

Higo 10c Store, Jackson near 6th—Imagine a kaleidoscope of Japanese items merchandised in F. W. Woolworth style . . . fun to find the original Japanese treasures, like tiny parasols, among the commonplace . . . great for children.

Scandinavian Imports, 4th near Virginia—Very representative of Scandinavian objects . . . famous Christmas plates; Norwegian silver, pewter; crystal from Sweden, Denmark . . . cooking and painted ware.

Tobo, 12th S. near Main—Colorful Japanese shop of everything from stone lanterns to food supplies . . . small and hodge-podge . . .patronized extensively by Japanese colony.

SALVAGE STORES

(Stock solution: "Well—you can always plant ivy in it".)

Goodwill Industries, Lane St. near Rainier Ave.—You grab a grocery cart and roll into a help-yourself bargain store . . . never saw so many discards that look like possibilities.

Bottle Exchange, 14th & Yesler—This one's a sleeper . . . looks like 3 stories of old beer bottles . . . but stop and check for the big bubbly blue Mexican gin bottles . . . occasional soybean tubs . . . demijohns and other odd ones imaginative women can use.

Salvation Army, Pike Place Market & Pioneer Square—two smaller stores in 2 of our most colorful areas . . . once one of Seattle's most important banks, the Pioneer Square store sells 2nd hand everything but money.

St. Vincent de Paul, Fairview N. on Lk. Union—The greatest sideshow of them all . . . like a foreign bazaar of cluttered streets . . . noisy music . . . big signs proclaiming today's special . . . perched on the shore and over our "downtown" lake.

COFFEE (OR TEA) BREAK

(Some spots to look for when you stop for a breather.)

Ana Hedin, 5th near Union—Tiny modern Swedish café . . . all butter yellow, aqua, and copper pots . . . same cook and waitresses for 16 years that I know of . . . perfection of fine home-cooked food.

Calico Kitchen, Roy near Broadway E.—A charmer of a country pantry . . . chocolate cake, angel pie, eggnog pie—all to "die" over . . . ladylike luncheons of soup, hot dish or sandwich.

Frederick & Nelson Tearoom, Pine and 5th—Serve-yourself candle-lit tea table set up from 2:30 on . . . choice pastries, small sandwiches, salads—and tea, to rest for the next foray.

Rose Garden Tearoom, Westlake Alley & Pine—A real tearoom, all roses and crocheted doilies . . . but proud of their coffee and lemon chiffon pie . . . handwriting analyzed while-you-wait.

Ye Olde Ice Cream Parlor, 6th & Pine—Carriage Trade Sundaes and Super-Parfaits . . . but fuel for more shopping . . . conveniently in the middle of everywhere.

BOOK STORES

Hartman's, two stores, 5th near Pine, and on University Way —Good reputation and large selection . . . University store invites you to read by the fireplace . . . both serve coffee.

University Book Store, University Way near 45th—Hub of activities on the "Avenue" . . . store has grown beyond books, but it still has an outstanding section and selection.

Archway, Pike near 4th—New and shiney modern . . . number 1 paperback supply in town . . . a huge store.

Shorey's, 3rd near Marion—One of the largest dealers in 2nd hand books in the country—over ½ million in stock . . . a browser's paradise.

John Knaide, E. Pine near Broadway E.—Second hand and rare books in a natural setting of antique furniture—which also is collected for sale.

Bookmart, Pike near 6th—You'll have trouble wending your way through, but Mr. Stoops, a character in his own right, knows location of every book. Collectors like this one.

SOME FOOD SPECIALISTS

Brenner Bros. Bakery, 23rd & Cherry—For bagels (600 doz. a week) . . . hearth baked breads, lox, corned beef, Aunty Ada's dill pickles . . . and Yetta, the most glamorous bakery maiden in town.

Angelo's, Burien—For sourdough French bread flown in weekly from SF . . . gourmet foods and food specialties from everywhere . . . a character spot where you also can wine and dine.

Vyvey's, Bothell Way & 80th—For Belgian cottage bread, Old Country bread . . . large wine stock, domestic and imported . . . an unusual shop of everything related to food . . . a gourmet's delight.

Italian Market, Pike Place Market—For all Italian specialties . . . buckets of pastas . . . wonderful cheese . . . across from an herb nook.

Swiss Pastry Shop, 5th near Union—For brioche, croissants, French pastries that are positively sinful . . . Dutch chocolates, rum cakes . . . Swiss novelties and memorabilia.

La Mexicana, White Center—For homemade tortillas . . . tostados, the makings for chili . . . they *might* make you a taco to eat whilst there.

Fish markets, Alaskan Way Pier 51-56—For really fresh fish within a fishing line of their habitat . . . we like the Alaska black cod, halibut cheeks, clams for steaming—and the Dungeness crab . . . and you can ship a whole salmon anywhere.

FOR THE FRIEND WHO HAS EVERYTHING

(Some of the "onlys" and "bests" in Seattle)

Mounted animal life—Jonas Bros, E. Pine & Boylston, is the world's biggest taxidermist . . . game shipped in from all over the world to be mounted.

Airplane skis—Washington Aircraft, Boeing Field, sells the finest skis made—for airplanes, that is.

Artificial eyes—Erickson Laboratories, Med. Dental Bldg. are the only manufacturers of artificial eyes west of Chicago.

Ship's wheels—Few places left where a custom made ship's wheel can be bought . . . try Karl Seastrom, Lk. Washington Ship Canal.

Totem poles—From 2 inches to 30 feet at the Old Curiosity Shop, Pier 52 . . . or custom carved by Dudley Carter, one of the NW outstanding craftsmen—his examples are in prominent spots all over town.

CHILD CARE

(Some downtown nurseries for small fry during shopping. All are well equipped with play things, provide supervision, and hot lunches.)

Medical Dental Bldg. Nursery, Olive Way near 6th—Open 9 am-5 pm, in shadow of the Monorail on the Mall.

Cobb-Stimson Bldg. Nursery, 4th & University—called the drive-in nursery through the garage under the bldg.

Child Play Center, 8th near Olive Way—open 7:30 am-6 pm Sat. too . . . nap facilities and kindergarten.

SOME HINTS FROM THE EXPERTS

Gunderson's, Pine near 6th—For fine antique jewelry, and we know what outstanding designing they do . . . small and perfect.

Crissey's, 5th near Union—The most artistic in flowers and arrangements come from Crissey's . . . a lovely shop to investigate.

85

Corner Cupboard, University near 5th—Gift shop operated by the Orthopedic Hospital . . . well selected merchandise . . . staffed by pleasant volunteers.

Alexander-Charles Ltd. 5th near University—One of the few remaining shirtmakers in America . . . fit and fabrics will spoil a man for store-boughten shirts.

Elyse'e Fabrics, Union near 5th—great rolls of beautiful materials displayed like wallpaper . . . all imported fabrics . . . Pattern Lounge for the next step.

Standard Record, 65th near Roosevelt Way—Because they have such a large business, they discount record album sales . . . and because they discount record album sales, they have such a large business . . . probably most total selection in town.

Italian Shop, Broadway E. near Roy—A habit of Seattle women with discriminating taste . . . lovely imported gifts of every category.

John Uitti, University Way near 42nd—We do as many NW artists do . . . just take it to John Uitti and know that it will be framed absolutely *right* . . . a real individualist.

Bamboo Hut, Security Market on 4th—For that secret weakness of most women, baskets . . . a tremendous collection from all over the world . . . and many other treasures for the imaginative decorator.

Anne Itkin, Broadway E. near Roy—For beautiful linens and other boudoir accessories to make a woman feel properly pampered.

Pipe Lane, Pine near 6th—The complete tobacconists . . . all imported cigarettes . . . pipes and accessories.

John Rigali, 714 24th S.—Repairs clocks, but the attraction is his collection of over 1000 clocks . . . only 3 people can squeeze in at a time to see them . . . all running and strike at the same time.

Hardy's, Pine St. near 5th—Oldest quality jewelry store in Seattle . . . third generations are now buying *their* engagement rings sentimentally there. Gem specialists.

Osborn & Ulland, 2nd and Spring—Nationally known skiers, ski experts, and ski-equippers.

NORTHWEST COLOR

(For things typical of Seattle life—either the waterfront, some native crafts, or NW artists.)

Seattle Ship Supply, Fishermen's Terminal—Shuttles of yew wood, nylon rope in brilliant colors, fish net bags . . . ship models, bandanna hankies—even Hoochy Koochy Plastic Tails.

Fisheries Supply Co. Pier 55—Need a crab trap? . . . maybe bronze fittings for household novelties . . . out of the ordinary weather togs.

Ye Olde Curiosity Shop, Pier 52—Charles Dickens would never recognize it . . . world famous for curios . . . from wooden Indians, native baskets, totem poles . . . Swiss cowbells, Spanish hurdy gurdy . . . tie-dyed, fringe-edged souvenir pillows about "MOTHER" . . . in a row along here are several other shops of a similar but lesser nature.

Mack's Totem Curio Shop, Marion St. Viaduct—Ivory carvings in all colors . . . buttons, key rings, earrings . . . mineral specimens . . . Eskimo and Indian dolls . . . shell goods. And along this overhead walk from the waterfront are more unusual businesses.

Northwest Artists and Craftsmen—Art experts from elsewhere are struck by the reflection of our relaxed personality and spiritual contentment of living revealed in the "strong" work of our artists and craftsmen. As one man from the East said, "You are strong in a *nice* way. There isn't the 'push me, pull you' quality to be found in so many other places." And there are few cities where so much local work is found in public buildings and private homes. And we point with pride to Mark Tobey, Morris Graves, and Kenneth Callahan, our internationally famous trio.

To buy NW paintings, drawings, etc.: Dusanne Gallery, 532 Broadway E.; Little Gallery, Frederick & Nelson; Otto Seligman Gallery, 4710 University Way; Woessner Gallery, 4001 Beach Drive.

To buy works of NW craftsmen and designers: Keeg's, 1819 Olive Way; Miller-Pollard, 4538 University Way; Panaca, Bellevue Square, Bellevue—a new art and craft outlet, exclusively featuring 70 NW artists.

AFTER DARK

"Olive? Who's Olive?" "Our daughter, silly!"
From the Groucho Marx, Madeline Carroll
radio show

I think of the above quotes whenever I mention the word "Night Life" in Seattle and get the reaction: "Night life? What night life?"

Most Seattleites reflect the question of the world traveler who had been given a scenic daytime tour of our city. He is reported to have asked, "Very nice. But what do you do when the sun goes down?"

Some of our more conservative citizens reply with, "That's not a proper question to ask a lady!" Others cynically reply, "We watch television."

We're slightly inhibited by the fact ours is the only town in the world that had a university before it had a house of prostitution. The fact is the "bawds" from San Francisco arrived in Puget Sound country looking over the most likely spot for an operation and settled on Seattle as the best prospect 20

88

years before the railroad moguls finally came to the conclusion we were going to be *the* important city.

We ran so high, wide and handsome on night life in our earlier years that the citizens clamped down on things.

The lid lifted considerably after the First War when Art Hickman wrote the song "Rose Room" after the room by the same name in the flagrantly jazzy Butler Hotel (now a garage). We had rum runners running rum in from Canada on signals from children's bedtime stories over one of our major radio stations.

The training acquired by some of our best mechanics in keeping the rum boats in top trim, now is being put to effective use in keeping the hydroplanes running during the "unlimited" races during Seafair on Lake Washington.

The "Puget Sound Cocktail" was a name wryly developed during those hectic days. A boat load of whiskey hit a log boom and sank with about $10,000 worth of liquid goods aboard.

A diver recovered the goods and everybody settled down for a victory drink only to discover the bottles were half-filled with sea water.

Our night life went into dark days during the 30's and '40's when either private clubs or the movies had a corner on it. In the '50's television monopolized the scene.

But there have been too many dead cowboys . . . and six-shooters that shoot 16 shots without re-loading, and the adhesive of novelty that once glued our eyes to anything on television has worn off.

We've become unglued. The same spirit that enabled John Considine and Alexander Pantages to control the nation's two great vaudeville circuits from a little Northwest town—pop. 80,000—has re-emerged.

The high cost of domestic help . . . the burned meat in the backyard barbecues . . . the dreadful business of cleaning the "boat" after an expensive weekend of entertaining guests—plus excellent entertainment in our restaurants—have pushed us into a pattern that goes like this:

Dinner out. (There is such a variety of choice in restaurants, you can dine as expensively or inexpensively as you like, depending on the state of your pocket book).

Then to the Symphony (one of the best in the United States) . . . or to the legitimate theater (with a wide choice of plays and more than adequate talent) . . . or bar-hopping (we like to take one drink in each spot and move on, and we find a lot of others doing the same) . . . or dancing on a small scale, though, like elsewhere, this is a fading fancy.

Unlike a few years back, we find the ladies in snug, low-cut evening clothes—whether they're in one of the smart uptown cocktail lounges or down at the joyous jazz-and-beer joints on the skidroad. (We even have female impersonators at one night spot.)

We also have variety in foreign films . . . or good downtown movies since the movie industry has learned the lesson "teevee" is learning. And since our last book, there has been an interesting outcropping of off-beat coffee houses.

But don't take my word for it. Become a true sophisticate . . . Become a happy human being for a few hours by trying any collection of the following:

LITTLE THEATERS

(For current information about each of these categories, see the weekly Seattle Guide.)

The University of Washington Group—probably the only university in the U.S. operating 3 little theaters for the public year round:

Penthouse—UW Campus. Designed by Prof. Glenn Hughes in 1932, this is the first playhouse in the world built for drawing room plays in circus style. Now copied internationally. Name came from original location in penthouse of Meany Hotel.

Showboat—Ft. of 15th N.E. & U.W. Campus. One of the most picturesque playhouses in America. Built to resemble a vessel on shore of Portage Bay. Has revolving stage for rapid scene changes.

University Playhouse—E. 41st & University Way. For unusual productions of an artistic nature . . . has one of the most modern stage-lighting systems in the country . . . notable for ability to project scenic designs.

Note: Our Drama Department is recognized throughout the nation as one of the most outstanding and best-equipped allowing the greatest freedom of experience.

Cirque Playhouse—34th & East Union. You'd never know it now, but this once was a garage for repairing automobiles. It has come about its present importance under the driving energy of director-manager-owner-actor-entrepreneur-painter-carpenter Gene Keene. Usually has a Hollywood star in the "lead", but Gene will pick anybody that seems a likely prospect.

Boards Playhouse—5011 Calif. Ave. This offers anyone interested in any phase of the legitimate stage from stage-hand to leading lady an opportunity for self expression. Very successful.

Old Seattle Theater—1st & Madison—At one time this was one of the nation's most important vaudeville acts. As the city moved north, vaudeville died. Our last strip tease burlesque died here a couple of years ago . . . the same year that 1,500,-000 people visited Mt. Rainier (an interesting commentary on what we think is beautiful). Now a part of a major movement to restore old Seattle, this theater is operated, acted in by people who have other jobs but just can't resist the lure of the Theater . . . and their productions are very good.

FOR ROAD SHOWS

Moore-Orpheum-Palomar—Their future as stages for legitimate theater is dubious. When comes the end of Century 21, more modern facilities will be available. However, at the moment, road shows use these. The Moore and Palomar are a part of historic Seattle. Mr. Moore was one of the great entrepreneurs who helped build the city. The Palomar was once a big moment in the life of a Greek immigrant named Pericles (nee Alexander) Pantages, vaudeville mogul, who signified he'd reached a plateau in his career by naming a theater after himself. The Orpheum presently "houses" the Seattle Symphony and our main road shows. The rest of the time it shows movies.

Note: We modestly point out that the Seattle Symphony Or-

91

chestra, which is moving to the new Opera House in spring, 1962, is listed as one of the nation's major symphony orchestras. Born in 1903, it really began to come into flower in 1954 with Milton Katims, who is as much of a hero, believe-it-or-not, as Bob Schloredt who quarterbacked two U.W. Rose Bowl championship teams. At one time we had a most unpleasant experience with the late Sir Thomas Beecham, who shook us by the neck until our teeth rattled during his short span as conductor here. We have been trying ever since to explain he didn't mean it when he said, "Seattle is an aesthetic dustbin." Fortunately, Sir Thomas, himself, made his amends in 1960, just prior to his death, by hearing our orchestra and remarking with his usual candor: "I must tell you, you have a very fine orchestra here. Preserve and cherish it. No asset is more indicative of the high culture of a community."

Aqua Theater—Greenlake. Outdoor theater with water between the audience and the stage. Used in summer only for Aqua Follies . . . musicals. (It was on approximately this site that Sarah Bernhardt went bear-hunting half-a-century ago. Our fun-loving forefathers unleashed a tame bear from behind some bushes. Sarah sighted him with her gun, noted the worn spot where his collar had been and didn't shoot. She did, however, blow a fuse at this kind of a mean trick, but finally was mollified when she was permitted to bag some honestly wild ducks.)

UP TOWN BAR HOPPING

Bar hopping in some of our uptown restaurants has become a favorite after-dinner Seattle habit. All of these bars are connected with a top restaurant or hotel. All of them have excellent musical entertainment. We usually stop for one drink in each place to get a variety of music and atmosphere during the evening.

Here are some of the best:

Rosellini's Four-10—usually has the best "group" in town, three or four men and a girl . . . always hilarious entertainment.

Dublin House—for Irish coffee around the piano bar in the Snuggery . . . high-ceilinged elegance.

Victor's 610—Another "group" type of entertainment in an informal Italo-French atmosphere.

Red Carpet—Usually ballad music being listened to by happy couples in intimate little nooks.

Cloud Room—On top of the Camlin Hotel, with outdoor terrace in good weather and wonderful view of city through huge plate glass windows during the winter.

Other good bets each with a different but sophisticated styling are: *Canlis . . . Viceroy . . . Marine Room . . . Orchard Room . . . Bib 'N Tucker . . . Captain's Table . . . Golden Lion.*

DANCING

Although the day of the big dance bands seems to have gone by the boards, we do have some small and intimate dancing spots like:

The Four Winds—Dinner dancing to Bob Harvey, band leader around here for 25 years . . . no need for "sea legs", even though this is a ship on Lake Union.

Norselander—Dinner dancing . . . swing and old Goodman groove . . . overlooking Puget Sound.

Porterhouse Eagle Inn—in Kenmore . . . dancing Fri. Sat. Sun. one of the joyous places . . . generally a Tahitian atmosphere

93

with lots of intimate pools, nooks and crannies . . . setups.

Dave's Fifth Avenue—Well now, if you like it lively, this is your spot . . . hot swing . . . cha cha . . . jazz . . . door charge.

Downbeat—Colorful spot off Pioneer Square . . . one of the fresh new spots attracting crowds to heart of old Seattle that offers dancing . . . door charge.

Magic Inn—Theater restaurant . . . featured acts booked here in addition to the dancing . . . door charge.

Casbah—Supper club, in the New Washington Hotel . . . decor is just what the name implies . . . popular spot.

Colony—Supper club . . . good jazz orchestra . . . show featuring "Fantasia" who dances and removes excess clothing gracefully.

BEER WITHOUT SKITTLES

These places may lack skittles, but they make up for them a thousandfold if you have an ounce of imagination and adventure in your soul. There's wine if you don't like beer.

Blue Banjo—Famous old Seattle saloon restored to its Gay Nineties glory, including a long . . . long . . . long bar . . . served up with straw hats, community singing and some of the best Dixieland jazz you ever heard . . . usually jam-packed with youngsters from 21 to 91 years of age. Pioneer Square. Door charge.

Gabe's—U-shaped bar with excellent stereophonic music and huge earphones if you like to listen to the music in private.

Golden Horseshoe—Don't go there if you can't stand female impersonators . . . but don't stay away if you're from uptown and hear it's on the Skidroad . . . you'll have plenty of "your kind" around you . . . the "boys?" "girls?" are clever.

Louie's—Same formula and same ownership as Banjo . . . separated from one another by pawn shop . . . original Seattle store fronts in basement from before the fire when the street level was one story lower . . . Roaring '20's brand of jazz. Door charge.

Pete's Poop Deck—original Skidroad jazz joint . . . he advertizes "covered" parking—the "cover" is the Alaskan Way Viaduct . . . avoid parking across the tracks . . . switch engines come by nightly . . . you sit on boxes at carved-up tables . . . *avant guard* jazz. Door charge.

Round Table—Uptown again . . . jazz piano bar . . . long tables . . . benches . . . and burlap . . .request music solicited.

Shakeys—On Bothell Way but worth the trip to find out what the younger generation enjoys . . . you get the point of the decor if you look at the picture inside above the front door —it is captioned "our founder" very reverently . . . and is framed with a toilet seat.

Place Pigalle—Pike Place Market . . . most unselfconsciously colorful spot in town . . . posters, drippy candles, bums, the longshore and tennis shoe crowd . . . and they *have* skittles here. If you swear here you have to give a contribution to the Children's Orthopedic Hospital.

COFFEE HOUSES

There's a rash of these, mostly frequented by the college crowd because there isn't all that bother of furnishing false I.D. to prove that people under 21 are over 21. But you won't be alone if you are over 21. The pattern of most coffee houses is to serve many varieties of coffees, continental type pastries, and exhibit local art. Many are open on Sundays too.

The Door—7th Ave. . . . Very off beat . . . usually has jazz.

El Matador—on a dock on Lake Union . . . Spanish guitar music.

Guenter's Pastry Shop—near U.W. campus . . . German with Tahitian atmosphere . . . good pastries and soft pretzels.

Encore—near U.W. campus . . . our original coffee house . . . Victorian decor.

The Place Next Door—next door to Guild 45th St. (foreign films) Theater . . . colorful—occasionally folksingers.

Pamir House—near U.W. campus . . . folksingers on weekends . . . very popular with the younger crowd . . . go if you feel young.

Vienna Kaffeehaus—next to Ridgmont (foreign films) Theater . . . Vienna coffees and pastries . . . dancing—waltzes, polkas, schottisches.

LATE NIGHT SNACKS, STEAKS, EGGS

Alpine Cafeteria—4th Ave. . . open 24 hours, 7 days . . . ham and eggs, and such cake! . . . after-hours crowd including many entertainers.

Boeing Cafeteria—near Plant 2 . . . open 24 hours . . . biggest cafeteria you ever saw . . . public welcome.

Elroy's—*Pioneer Square* . . . Gay 90's atmosphere and piano . . . try Suzuki Roma—spaghetti and meat balls served with chopsticks . . . fabulous hot dogs.

George's—6th Ave. . . . always open . . . long time Seattle landmark and favorite of ours for late snacks.

New York Bakery—Skidroad . . . on one of Seattle's few remaining board sidewalks . . . bums, police, homburg hats enjoying *good* coffee and rolls . . . closes at midnight.

Von's—4th Ave. . . . last of our fine old restaurants . . . 24 hours 7 days . . . after theater crowd . . . excellent steaks, eggs, and lemon meringue pie.

Italian Spaghetti House and Pizzeria—Bothell Way . . . one of few places in town where they still "toss" pizza . . . great spaghetti menu—7 different ways.

Do It Yourself Entertainment

The "see" in Seattle...

One of the devices we use in fund-raising campaigns is to tack a dollar bill to the undersides of the chairs of the volunteer solicitors at the kick-off banquet. The master of ceremonies concludes the meeting by asking everyone to get up and turn his chair over.

Then he says, "You see, if you'll just get up and move—there is no telling what will happen."

There are a lot of people who live in the Pacific Northwest but never "see" it. There are others who come here with a desire to see but need guidance. The following suggestions require a little more energy than turning the switch of a television set, but they also will be more rewarding:

LAND TOURS

Gray Line Tours—There is no Seattleite who wouldn't increase his knowledge of his city by about 90% if he would take one of these—except for the men who "lecture" the tours. The information provided has been thoroughly researched and sparkles with anecdotes like the one about the polar bear born in the Woodland Park Zoo who refuses to go near the water.

For an overall and interesting picture of the city fast, this is your cup of tea.

Trident Tours—Most of us have noticed the neat blue and green trident tour signs around the city. There are 400 of them . . . erected in 1958 to mark four different routes by which you can cover the city in your own automobile. If you shoot the works you cover 107 miles in chunks of 28, 21, 30 and 28, but you know the city better. Start from downtown, preferably with a pamphlet from the Tourist Information Bureau of the Chamber of Commerce, 215 Columbia (non-ticketed temporary curb-parking while you run in).

Residential Tours—A lot of visitors are tremendously interested in our gardens and interesting residences. We probably have more architect-designed homes than any city in the country. There shortly will be a new book by Victor Steinbrueck, Professor of Architecture at the University of Washington on our architecture, which should be a "must" if you're interested in this sort of thing.

If you're reading this after March, 1962, his book is already out. Meanwhile, here's his succinct statement on architecture: "The unique characteristics of today's Seattle Architecture are these: Freedom of expression encouraged by the newness of the country, design for a mild climate and soft rainfall averaging 32 inches annually, varied and skillful use of wood, adaptation to hilly topography and orientation to beautiful views of many snow-capped mountains, innumerable lakes and inlets of Puget Sound."

Try the hills and waterfronts, not the hollows.

WATER TOURS

Sightseer—Here's another Gray Line production that is a boat with loudspeakers and music interspersed by commentary. One trip each day each way from Leschi Park to Pier 56 through the locks. Nice restaurants—the Cove and Bob's Landing at each terminus and snacks on the boat. June through mid-September.

Harbor Tourist and Wave—If you've never seen our harbor from a small boat, you've never seen our harbor. These are sturdy little craft with outdoor viewing in good weather and

98

glass enclosed viewing otherwise. Trips take an hour. Summer season only. Loudspeaker commentary. Pier 55.

AIR TOURS

If you have the time and the money, you can charter a small seaplane at any one of a number of places on our "downtown" Lake Union or on Elliott Bay. We're a geographically spectacular area and these planes can take you "closer in" and slower than a commercial airliner.

WALKS

Saltwater Strip—From Yesler Way to University Street along the waterfront. A six block walk with all of the color and saltwater smell of an active waterfront concentrated in one small section . . . including three sidewalk "seafood bars" if the walk whets your appetite.

Arboretum—One for the whole family and nice places to picnic. Suggest you stop by the Arboretum office to find out what's "best" at the time you're here, and take time to really "do" the Japanese Tea Garden.

U.W. Campus—Suggest you have some kind-hearted person drop you at 17th N.E. and E. 45th, and then pick you up at the East Pacific-Montlake Boulevard entrance. That way it's a downhill pull. You probably can get a map from the gate house. Head for the Frosh Pond and the vista of Mt. Rainier, which the whole campus is more or less pointed toward.

Park Hiking—The following parks provide a nice challenge to the heel-and-toe treatment: Schmitz, only virgin forest tract in any U.S. city . . . Carkeek, a wild black bear has been spotted here in the last couple of years . . . Seward, with a fish hatchery and duck preserve . . . Lincoln, wonderful Puget Sound vistas . . . Woodland, and a zoo too. All of them are about 200 acres, have fine paths and are good leg stretchers if you're a leg stretcher. Picnic facilities everywhere.

Fishermen's Terminal—You can do a lot of interesting walking on these broad piers and most of the year see the boats that make up the world's biggest working fishing fleet. The "overheards" in the Wharf Restaurant coffee shop in the mornings are worth several extra cups of coffee. And don't miss browsing in the ship chandleries.

Government Locks—About 7 acres of garden and lots of dramatic activity in the raising and lowering of the boats. For those pangs of hunger we recommend Lavery's By The Locks. Two connected buildings—the original cookshack for the lock's construction crew . . . one of Ballard's oldest homes. It's said Harry Tracy, famous N.W. gunman held the owner's wife hostage overnight here. Quaint, interesting, unique. Beer . . . Seafood.

The Houseboats—I guess they are more or less unique to Seattle. Generally along the east side of Lake Union and around Portage Bay. Inhabited by uninhibited and friendly individualists and the houses show it. Saunter along the connecting piers or floats and see how the happy half of our population lives.

Fifth Avenue Axis—A "T" beginning at University Street and the Olympic Hotel (our biggest by far) and topped by Pine Street and the Westlake Mall. Some of our finest shops are in this general area. Suggest a return treat on Fourth Avenue.

INDUSTRIES THAT LIKE PEOPLE

I have a strong suspicion that most of the major industries around town would welcome visitors if the proper approach was made on the subject ahead of time. The Seattle Chamber of Commerce has a list of Plant Tours. So does the Audio-Visual Department of Seattle Public Schools.

Here are some suggestions from the two lists that make up a cross section we think is both interesting and educational: *Boeing-Renton*—Mondays, 8:15 p.m. phone in advance, JU 6-3192. Biggest manufacturers of airplanes in the world. Supply 40% of free world.

Continental and Langendorf Bakeries—Bread etc. 9:30-10:30 a.m. daily at the former and Mon. Wed. Thurs. Fri. at latter.

Imperial Candy Company—Tues.-Thurs. 9-11 a.m., and I'd bet they give you a piece of candy.

Carnation Company—After 2 p.m. When I went there when I was in the eighth grade, I got a dish of ice cream.

Elliott Bay Mill Company—One of our huge lumber mills . . they also saw up Philippine mahogany.

Sick's Rainier Brewing Company—Mon. thru Fri., 10 a.m. to 5 p.m. And I *know* you get a drink of beer.

KING Broadcasting Company—Sat. & Sun. 12n to 8. Radio-TV

Seattle Times & P.I.—Former, 1:30 to 3 p.m. . . . latter to 4 p.m. Mon. Thurs. Fri. All the drama of big daily newspapers.

Tsue-Chong Company—They make Chinese noodles and fortune cookies at 801 King St. and like to have you call in advance.

BICYCLING

The only place we know of you can rent bicycles are a couple of shops near Green Lake, but that's a pretty good place to rent bicycles because you can ride them around the lake. You get a nice outdoor experience in pleasant suroundings and the pumping is entirely on the level.

VIEWS

Smith Tower—Our most traditional place to go for views. Seattle's oldest space needle—42 stories. Price 50 cents.

Volunteer Park Water Tower—Dandy view of the Sound, etc. No charge except the exertion of climbing 288 steps.

Northern Life Tower—No charge, but stop in management office for passes.

Space Needle—Oh yes, that right. Really quite new—and very high. Price not quoted yet at this printing but I think it will be $1.25 for adults to the observation tower. It won't be hard to find.

* * *

PARK FACILITIES & PLAYGROUNDS

We have 3,500 acres of parks in our park system which originally was intended to have a park within walking distance of any home in the city. There are picnic places . . . beaches . . . concerts . . . boating areas . . . supervised play . . . camps . . . archery . . . lawn bowling . . . tennis . . . golf . . . boulevards . . . scenic trails and views . . . classes in all sorts of vocations.

The Park Department has a pamphlet which lists the location of every park, what bus to take if you can get there on a bus, in addition to a map and a chart showing what facilities are available at each park, playground and fieldhouse.

OTHER ODDS AND ENDS

There's the fireboat practice during summer months at the foot of Madison on Tuesdays about 2 . . . a naval reserve submarine to be visited at the south end of Lake Union . . . Coastguard lighthouses at Alki Point and West Point—all with visiting hours and you are welcome.

* * *

"A picnic is a state of mind . . ." Shirley Speidel

PICNICS AND FOOD TO MATCH

In my opinion the Pacific Northwest is one large, unrivalled picnic ground. I'm not necessarily referring to the kind where several families get together on a hot summer Sunday and load up a table in one of our parks . . . nor am I confining the idea of a picnic to the summer months.

We had a picnic recently in Lakeview Cemetery, where we certainly were in good, if quiet, company . . . most of our pioneer families have come to their resting place there. We've picnicked in the fog down at Gray's Harbor . . . and to the tune of winter storms in the shelters at Golden Gardens and Saltwater State Park. We had to drive 60 miles out of Pasadena to picnic under a Joshua tree at nightfall in the Mojave Desert. (We were worried about the possibility of poisonous animal life so we ate in the car—a little detail we wouldn't have worried about up here.)

We have a complete assortment of rivers, lakes, saltwater beaches and view sites in which to have a picnic. We can arrive at a picnic spot in 15 minutes or within an hour. And except on rare occasions we can picnic any time of the year.

Now about the food: Vyvey's . . . Stalders . . . where you can get one sandwich with 5 different kinds of meat and 2 of cheese . . . Brenner Brothers . . . Frederick's . . . the Bon . . .

Angelo's . . . and half a dozen other bakery-delicatessen shops have all of the necessary ingredients for a perfect picnic. We like finger foods and think a bottle of wine is a happy thought. One of our friends firmly believes it isn't a picnic unless you cook *something* on the spot. But we consider it one without cooking—even if we have it on our own front steps.

And, hey, how about Ivars, the Cove, or some of the other fish places where you can pick up food? Pizza and Chinese places all have food to go on a picnic with . . . or a browse through the Pike Place Market could put you in the proper mood with some dandy food.

It is even possible to cook your own fried chicken in your own motel room—or even your home!

You can build your own fire at most of our beaches and there are arrangements for fires in scads of State and Federal parks within an hour's drive.

A picnic is a state of mind, but we have the food here and a decent destination in a decently short interval at any point on the compass . . . so why not subject yourself to adventure?

* * *

PACIFIC NORTHWEST FOOD

Our Sea Fare and Land Fare and Your Welfare

A hundred years ago the apple, which is a crop that crops up in a lot of conversations here, wasn't getting any "play" at all in Seattle. It had to be brought in from San Francisco, and the price down there ranged from 25c to $5—*per apple*.

Today, we're the largest single apple-producing area in the world. And Wenatchee is the biggest apple locale in the state. When I was a kid they had a contest for a slogan to advertise their apples. I always got a kick out of the simplicity of the winning slogan. It was: "Eat Wenatchee Apples!"

The Lord provided places like Wenatchee-Yakima with ideal apple-growing conditions—a heavily mineralized soil of glacial till, volcanic ash, river sediment . . . warm days and cool nights with a plentiful supply of irrigation water. There are 68,000 square miles inside the state boundaries . . .

65,000 acres of apples . . . 31,000 carloads a year are shipped out to all parts of the world . . . that's two billion five hundred million apples . . . wow! Income to the state from the apple crop averages $100,000,000 a year.

Most people don't seem to, but if you do go broke in the apple country, the state makes you cut down all your trees and dispose of them. It seems like adding insult to injury, but an untended orchard means infestation . . . and that means trouble for everybody else.

We grow some luscious cherries, too. And a rainstorm at about picking time is as about as welcome as a visit from the mother-in-law of your divorced wife. I like the story of the farmer who hired a helicopter to hover over his orchard after such a storm to dry off his cherries and keep them from splitting.

Wheat is our top crop, with milk and apples in there pitching for second or third place every year. We're really a land of milk and honey, and the bees are businessmen hired out at so much a day to pollenize our orchards.

We're one of the nation's major mint producing areas—growing a brand with one flavor east of the mountains and another west of the mountains. And the chances are if you've chewed some spearmint gum lately the flavor came from here.

The Lord had trouble making up an exact location for our ocean shores. He wavered back and forth from the Cascade Mountains in, say, the last few million years. In the process He left behind some bogs near our ocean shores that are ideal for cranberries. If you should take a trip to the ocean, take a look at those bogs. The trimly-kept cranberry bogs are some of the most valuable pieces of property in the world . . . about a thousand acres in the Long Beach-Grays Harbor area.

We lead the nation in processing peas . . . we're second only to California in our strawberry crop—but we think ours have more flavor than theirs. We have about 3,000 acres in red raspberries—most of which go into frozen foods, which got their start in this state. We have a lot of huckleberries, and their greens are almost as important for floral decorations as the berries . . . combination of the two is a $5,000,000 annual industry. Blueberries are coming up as a major crop.

Sadly, the currants, which make currant jelly which made my life more pleasant as a child, are fading from the market for lack of demand. The last stronghold seems to be Vashon Island where this book is being written . . . and I don't think it's very strong. You should see the fields of currants that are going to weeds on Vashon.

You can't eat 'em . . . but you can go to Palm Springs in the winter if you own enough Christmas trees. These we ship all over the world . . . a very profitable crop.

Altogether, we're one of the best berry sections in the country. If you're a visitor be sure and con somebody into buying you a piece of wild blackberry pie. Put some ice cream on it and you'll have had something you'll never forget.

We ship out about 500 tons of berries a year.

We're famous for our seafood, with salmon leading the economic pack . . . and we're the most important halibut port in the world.

We try to time trips to a luncheon or dinner stop at the Oyster House in Olympia for a pan-fry of Olympia oysters, the most succulent marine bivalve mollusk the world has ever known. They're done in butter . . . and be specific that you don't want them gooped up with tomato sauce.

You'll have to hock your watch to buy a round of these for

105

the family, but then again it's a taste treat you may never experience again. I don't know whether the Olympics are winning or losing against the pollution from the pulp mills these days, but there's been a pretty energetic running fight on this subject for some time.

To give you some idea of their size, there are between 500 and 600 Olympia oysters to the pint . . . 45 to 50 of the next smallest oyster I know of. You'll find that our best restaurants have a "pipeline" in to the yearling Quilcene oyster growers, a delicate dish if ever there was one. And if you're a friend of oysters, put some lime on the nearest starfish—they're the oyster's most vicious enemy and I never even tried to eat a starfish.

Recently a huge bed of tiny shrimp was found off the Washington coast . . . they clean them with high pressure nozzles (don't ask me how) . . . extremely tasty, though. And if you leave the state without tasting our Dungeness crab in season you don't belong to the gourmet group.

You'll probably have to have pull like they did to get a drink in the old speakeasy days, but smoked, kippered smelt "netted" or "dishpanned" in the Columbia River in season, is one of the world's great gastronomic adventures.

The truth is you can only eat so much salmon and halibut and their "poor" relations, the bottom fish . . . sole . . . sable fish . . . outclass them for flavor but haven't had the headlines. The Market Development Division of the Bureau of Commercial Fisheries holds taste tests with different recipes at about 11 o'clock each weekday morning in Ballard . . . and let us hope they will make a major break-through to the palates of the people one of these days. It'll mean more money to us and more taste treats to the "folks".

I wish I could say that anybody could go with shovel in hand and for the privilege of an hour's back-breaking labor acquire a mess of clams. But it isn't that easy. However, if you have "connections" you may find somebody with a "clam beach".

Usually, they will be delighted to hand you a shovel and let you go to work. Usually, also, they're such suckers for this delightful food item, they not only will assist you with the digging but dig out some cold beer which is a most welcome commodity when you get into this business.

106

Plan ahead to get your feet wet and your trousers muddy.

If you don't want to go to all this pleasure, clams are available, very fresh and quite reasonable at almost any fish market . . . and for real ease of acquiring this taste treat, try one of our many excellent "fish" houses.

I couldn't possibly include all of the food processing plants in the Northwest in this volume, but here are some that are interesting and important to our lives:

"ALA" Be Praised!

Recently, at about the time a gourmet friend of mine forked over 81¢ in excess weight to take a 29¢ package of ALA back to Rockford, Illinois on the plane with her because she couldn't find any in Illinois' 2nd largest city, Fisher Flouring Mills Company was sending a 1,000,000-pound shipment to Asia . . . they're shipping 5,000,000 pounds a month in the "Food For Peace" Program.

Here's an illustration of the kind of "company courage" that made Seattle the most important Pacific Northwest city and will keep us there. They don't know about ALA (Fisher's trade name for bulghour wheat) in Rockford, Ill. But this treatment of the wheat kernel (it's soaked, dried and cracked for quick, tasty cooking) has been in use in Asia over 3,000 years.

What does this mean to Seattle? Fisher's is the biggest U.S. manufacturer of this food. Our soft, eastern Washington wheat, not suitable for bread, is admirable for ALA. This means thousands of tons come to our port instead of being "barged" to Portland. With ocean shipping costs one-tenth of those over land, we're closer to Tokyo than Chicago in terms of economic distances. The third side of this triangle lies in the courage of Fisher's to complete, this year, the most modern flour mill in the world.

With the explosive growth of wealth in Asia, we will be in a dominant world position to supply the people there with a basic food product. It's a gourmet item to be found in our smart restaurants as pilaf—a replacement for those dreadful "french fries". It's a basic necessity over there.

You can find the attractive red, white, blue ALA package

in almost any grocery here. May we suggest you brown it in butter or bacon fat first, then follow package directions. If you try to boil it, you won't get pilaf.

And who knows? Maybe one day it will match the popularity of Fisher's Scones at the Puyallup Fair.

Our Favorite Flavor Factory . . .

Call it provincial if you like, but we quietly avoid grocery stores that don't carry Crescent seasoning and spices. And this doesn't mean that we're necessarily odd balls. The Seattle Times Consumer Analysis shows we're right in the groove with 53.9% of the folks.

The Times survey didn't get involved in a whole lot of other stuff, but it did concern itself with something as basic as pepper. And that's how their statistics showed up on this front.

I suppose that a lot of people figure that pepper is pepper . . . and instant minced onions by any other name are just as sweet. But the name "Crescent" on them has earned a special spot in our hearts.

Crescent is one of the reasons why Seattle is the major city in the Pacific Northwest. They were "burned out" by the fire in 1889. They employ about 200 people. They provide leadership in civic affairs. And they also turn out a superior product.

They subtly publicize the city of Seattle, for example, in the sale of Mapleine in 77% of the U.S. grocery stores. Mapleine, which permits American housewives to make inexpensive maple syrup, is a subject of distress to other extract manufacturers. Nobody has been able to "crack" the formula in over half a century.

This is more or less beside the point, but I am intrigued that Crescent sells more baking powder in Hong Kong than anyone else in the United States, but it has to be packaged in a red can instead of their usual blue because red means good luck in China.

And, to cap it all, I think it is simply splendid that a frontier lumbering village should give birth to one of the most important spice processors in the entire country.

Farman's—For getting pleasantly pickled . . ."

It pleases me to contemplate the fact that the second largest industry in Enumclaw is a pickle factory . . . the largest is the Weyerhaeuser Company (part of the biggest lumber company in the world). The second largest is the Farman Brothers Pickle Company.

I could survive my remaining days without touching any other kind of a pickle, but I doubt if I could last out next week without a dill pickle. And in my opinion, the Farman Brothers produce the best commercially packed dill pickles in the United States.

I evidently am not alone in this opinion because they sell a million quarts of their pickles annually. The Brothers, Fred and Dick, got into the pickle business in 1932 . . . the dills amount to about 40% of their sales.

The difference between Farman's and other commercially-packed dills is this: Most commercial pickle manufacturers salt their cucumbers down to hold them. Then when a dill pickle is needed, they cook the salt out, add the dill and other spices and you have dill pickles.

With Farman's, a cucumber destined to be a dill is barrelled with the necessary spices in the first place. This is possible in the Pacific Northwest because we don't have extremes in temperature that would ruin the aging process.

So chalk up another point for our mild climate, pickle-lovers, and add this one to your arguments when you tell your subway-sardine friends from the East about the natural wonders of the Pacific Northwest.

* * *

Signs of the times . . . Welcome to Milwaukee!

I can't resist including the Milwaukee Sausage Company in this volume. I probably shouldn't when I consider they have such signs on their Fourth Avenue South "Reader Board" as "Welcome, Tourists . . . This is Milwaukee!"

We wondered why a firm born, and bred in Seattle since 1916, would name itself after another city. The point is that at that time sausage, hot dogs, knockwurst, head cheese and the like were by-products of the normal meat-packing business. Only in Milwaukee was sausage-making the primary objective . . . and as a result the name had a better connotation . . . ergo, a Seattle firm named Milwaukee, with the primary purpose of making sausage.

They unquestionably produce a superior product, but where they have really endeared themselves to Seattleites is through the slogans on their reader boards. They have practically everybody in the city competing for an opportunity to have such items as the following posted on the boards—one on 4th S. and one on Aurora:

"I never sausage quality" . . . "the taste comes clean through the skin unseen" . . . "the wurst is yet to come" . . . "we make refrigerator door openers" . . . "no itsey bitsey teenie weenie" . . . "franks fer ter memory" "we make both ends meat" . . . "seven days without Milwaukee makes one weak" . . . "have a happy Hallowweenie" . . . "frank heaven for little grills" . . . and for the Christmas holidays, "Seasoned greetings". We also like some of the epic poetry, to-wit: "Split a bun and in be-tweenie put a sizzlin' Milwaukee weenie."

I sort of feel imagination like that above lightens the load of life and should be encouraged. The most encouraging thought I can offer is that you purchase their product. That will make them think we like them (Milwaukee & product).

As long as it's our book, we'll make our own suggestion for a board: "Backyard barbecue—the *bier* that made Milwaukee famous."

* * *

Keep Clam!

One of the great seafood products—found only in this corner of the world—is the razor clam, which beds down in ocean beaches from northern Oregon to the Aleutian chain. And I trust it won't be confused with any other clam in the world.

Unlike any other clam, it can move—*fast!* It lives alone and likes it. It can be detected by a small hole at the surface. You dig each clam individually, and you dig fast or it dis-appears. Your limit, in this state, is 18 clams and they're sup-posed to be 4½ inches long. Game keepers swarm the beaches helping to keep people "honest".

Its thin, gold and brown egg-shell quality shell looks like it belonged to the clam's younger brother because there is always more clam than shell. The meat is white, tender enough to cut with a fork and the flavor is far more delicate than that of the usual clam.

It has been packed under the label, "Pioneer Clams" since 1916 and presently is canned by Alaska Packers. The firm guarantees there is no sand in their cans and I guarantee you will have a taste treat if you have never tried them.

A million people a year dig these delicacies on Washington beaches, but the major commercial pack is centered around Cordova, Alaska. The commercial pack last year was 2,400,000 cans called "half-flats". All of them must be dug by hand, no dredging like on the east coast where clams are dredged at depths as much as 42 feet of water.

Anybody who has "busted his back" digging his quota of 18

will appreciate the robust effort of a man in Cordova who dug 1,469 pounds of clams on one tide. At present digging rates he would have made $220.35 for his "tide". (At the time he made the record he got 13c a pound or $190.97.)

You can get recipes from the packers. The clams are minced and make a wonderful white chowder or clam patties. The total crop is absorbed by Washington, Oregon and California, so if you're from the East you better stock up before returning.

* * *

Sea Fare . . . Our college-bred salmon

Like the recurring theme of a symphony, the impact of the University of Washington on the community and the impact of the community on the University, crops up on the matter of salmon.

We send salmon out to sea from our college pond in order to study their habits and advise our fishing industry. That industry, incidentally, has spent $2,000,000 in research at the University—and is the industry ever pleased with the results of their expenditure!

An example: The Fisheries Research Institute at the University predicted a big run of salmon in Bristol Bay in 1960. While the "catch" is made in 10 days or so, that isn't the entire story. Cans, personnel, equipment must be available to handle the catch—whatever it is. On the basis of the Institute's prediction, the salmon industry prepared for a big run.

Because of this preparation, the industry was able to can 5,000,000 more salmon than they had previously anticipated —a crop worth $12,000,000.

We're probably the biggest salmon port in the world—last year 45,000,000 salmon were distributed through Seattle. The Pacific Ocean yields about 20 times as many salmon as the Atlantic . . . the Japanese and Russians get about 60% of that catch . . . but mostly theirs is the poorer quality of salmon.

A salmon by any other name is just as nutritious, but I am astonished at the number of names there are for this fish. For example, a Chinook, Spring and King are all the same fish. Cohoe and a Silver is another pair of names meaning the same

112

thing. This also is true of the Pink and Humpy . . . the Blue-back, Sockeye and Red and the Chum and the Dog.

And they're all salmon.

* * *

How Now, Brown Cow?

Darigold is by far and away the most important dairy products concern in the Pacific Northwest. The Seattle Times Consumer Survey showed, for example, that 63.4% of their readers bought Darigold products. The next nearest choice was 6%.

Darigold does an annual gross business of about $125,-000,000. It is a cooperative owned by some 30,000 dairy farmers operating through 32 plants and 16 sub-stations in the four Pacific Northwest states.

A Lynden Chicken In Every Pot

Lynden is synonymous wih poultry in the Pacific Northwest. With headquarters in Seattle, it does about a $65-million business in three northwest states through 36 divisions.

It hits the national market with its canned—usually in glass—product featuring young, tender chicken . . . and the whole wishbone as an indication that the bird has not been cut up. It also was one of the leaders in the development of the broad-breasted turkey which has been copied all over the nation.

As A Matter of FACTS

An interpretation of the facts that may or may not be approved by the Seattle Chamber of Commerce ...

Name: "Queen City" of the Pacific Northwest.

Measurements: (In quarter miles). Bust 30, (West Point-Laurelhurst) ... Waist 10 (Yesler Way) ... Hips 28 (Alki-Seward Park) ... Height 64 (north-south city limits).

Age: 110 years ... or 108 years ... or 96 years ... or 92 years. (Pioneer founders landed in 1851 ... platted in 1853 ... incorporated in 1865 ... *disincorporated* in 1867 ... reincorporated in 1869).

Address: 47 degrees, 36 minutes. Geographic center of U.S. since statehood of Hawaii and Alaska? (Could be).

... 125 nautical miles from Pacific Ocean.

... 128 miles from Canadian border.

... 350 miles closer to Tokyo & London than San Francisco.

... 660 miles closer to Tokyo & London than Los Angeles.

... 33 miles north of Puyallup.

Telephone: More people talk on the telephone in Seattle than in any other city in the Pacific Northwest. (Long distance, because Seattle is the major city.) . . . First telephone call in 1878 was made from downtown to West Seattle and somebody goofed. Caller sought to commemorate the occasion by requesting a recitation of the "Lord's Prayer". The answer was, "Gee, mister, I don't know it. Would 'Now I Lay Me Down to Sleep' do?"

Nearly 400,000 telephones, all dial . . . headquarters for Pacific Telephone Bell.

Physical Condition: Excellent. One of the world's cleanest, best-lighted cities, thanks to a plentiful supply of water, steep grades for washing it off, and an abundance of electrical power.

. . . 91.6 square miles inside city limits, including 3.07 mi. of water, 192 miles of waterfront.

. . . built (Like Rome, we are wont to say) on 7 hills — Capitol, Magnolia, First, Queen Anne, Beacon, West Seattle, Denny. (Unlike Rome, we tossed one of the hills, Denny, into Puget Sound to make room for used car lots and motels. A movement now is under way to rebuild the hill.)

. . . altitude, sea level to 514 feet.

. . . generally a north-south city ground out by glaciers, with Olympic Mountains and Puget Sound on west and Cascades & 26-mile Lake Washington on east.

. . . 45,000,000 cubic yards of dirt taken from miscellaneous hills to fill in distressing hollows like 75-foot ravine in Seneca Street, bog under Frederick & Nelson, tideflats south of King Street.

. . . 91 bridges, with more coming, keep the whole thing hanging together.

. . . 36,000 street lights plus a growing tendency to return to the "living" gas lights of the gay nineties.

Previous Experience: Youngest major city in U.S., thanks to a quarter-billion-dollar boost from the Alaska gold rush & World War II.

. . . 70th largest city in U.S. in 1870, 19th largest today.
Population increase by decades:

1870—1,107	1920—315,000
1880—3,533	1930—365,000
1890—42,837	1940—368,000**
1900—80,671	1950—467,591***
1910—237,000*	1960—550,525****

. . . *increase 194% thanks to 8 annexations of 35 sq. mi.
& AYP.

. . . **deaths almost equalled births, virtually no in-migration.

. . . ***huge troop transports through Seattle served as in-
troduction to Seattle for thousands who returned later as
permanent residents.

. . . ****increase of nearly 100,000 while N.Y. and S.F.
populations fell off. (N.Y. by 100,000, S.F. by 30,000).

. . . Pop. center of city, 1900—Seventh & Cherry.

. . . Pop. center of city, 1960—Home of Guy Rockwell, former antique dealer just north of Fairview N. & Galer. Mr.
Rockwell presently unpopular with police over disappearance
of his ex-wife. House posted "Keep Out!"

. . . Pop. center of Seattle & Suburbs—St. Mark's Cathedral.

. . . Pop. density of city 6,250—densest pop. N. of S.F.

Aggressive Tendencies: Instigated purchase of Alaska.
. . . sent huge logs all over country to publicize our timber
resources. One of them, a squared-timber 111 feet long,
51 x 53 inches in diameter ended up as Chicago's longest bar.
. . . gave President Rutherford B. Hayes a log 150 feet long
when he was travelling Puget Sound in 86-foot boat.

. . . Started own railroad when N.P. made Tacoma its terminus. Made it pay.

. . . Sent man with wonderful name of "Orange" Jacobs to
Congress.

. . . Constitutional convention stalled three days over whether
or not "The Lord" should be named in preamble to constitution. "The Lord" forces won.

. . . "Grabbed *Gateway To Alaska* title with publicity gimmick. Steamer *Excelsior* arrived in S.F. from Alaska with $1,000,000 in gold in July 1897. Steamer *Portland* arrived Seattle with $500,000 worth of gold. We called ours a "ton of gold", got the traffic inbound and outbound from Alaska.

. . . 1888—spent $1,000 planting 1,000 trees in downtown streets, subsequently removed trees to make room for "progress".

. . . 1956—initiated program at cost of $31,000 to plant 750 trees in downtown streets. Trees still there.

. . . 1909—staged 14th World's Fair (AYP). First world fair to end in the "black".

. . . pledged $100,000 so Moran Bros. could get construction of battleship *Nebraska* (and then didn't pay the pledges).

Inferiority Complex: The WEATHER. One of the nine most pleasant places to live in the U.S. (Others are listed as Florida, Nevada, Arizona, California, New Mexico, Colorado, Utah, Hawaii.) But we spend most of our time pointing out the fact there is greater precipitation in 28 *other* U.S. cities than Seattle. More chauvinistic Seattleites have reached point of saying, "There is no rain in hell. If you don't like it here, why don't you go there?"

. . . extreme temperatures on record are 3 degrees & 100 F. But these are rare.

. . . average summer temperature 63 degrees (max. 70-75 degrees).

. . . average winter temperature 42 degrees (min. about 37 degrees).

. . . average rainfall 31.92" (mostly in winter).
Present employment: About 390,000 or about ½ of state employment.

. . . Home office of 19 Ins. Companies—two of them among the nation's largest, Northwestern Mutual and General.

. . . Home of world's largest manufacturer of aircraft.

. . . 2,000 ships (valued to us at $50,000 each) dock here yearly.

117

Personal Idiosyncrasies: People who live in apartment houses *must* eat some ice cream, because only 79.9% of us own our homes and 82.7% eat ice cream.

... more babies per 1,000 population survive than in any other U.S. city.

... World-famous Children's Orthopedic Hospital administered entirely by women.

... our electric rates are 40% of the national average and more people own their own electric stoves and water heaters than in any other U.S. city, regardless of size.

... one in six residents owns a boat big enough to be registered with the Coast Guard, making us the boating capital of the world.

... 200,000 people go skiing every year. We probably have more first class skiing areas closer to a major city than anywhere in the world.

... we have fewer millionaires, but more ½ millionaires than most major U.S. cities ... and houses costing $75,000 to $150,000 sell faster than houses costing $25,000.

... 49% of us own backyard barbecues and more people buy Chevrolets than Fords, although the race is close.

... Our drinking water is so pure that even fish can live in it, and practically nobody can make a living selling either bottled water or water softeners. We have an enormous supply of good clean water and our water rates are the lowest in the U.S.

... both our cost of living and our income is away above the national average.

... our municipally-owned electric system is one of the first in the country and is second only to Los Angeles in size.

... advent of natural gas in 1956 cut gas rates to home owners by one-third ... 85% of our restaurants cook with gas.

... our per capita fire loss is 60% below ... and our fatality loss is 75% below the national average.

... we have more women than men and they are better at figures.

... latest census figures available show the following characteristics:

Racial		Foreign Born	
White	—510,559	Canadian	—18,000 plus
Negro	—26,901	Norwegian	—10,000 plus
Native Indian	—1,729	Swedish	— 8,000 plus
Japanese	—9,351	English	— 7,000 plus
Chinese	—4,076	German	— 4,000 plus
Filipino	—3,755	Italian	— 3,000 plus
		Danish	— 2,000 plus
		Scotch	— 2,000 plus
		Russian	— 2,000 plus
		Finnish	— 2,000 plus

... with wealth comes whiskey. Only 30% of men earning under $4,000 drink whiskey. Of those earning $15,000, 84% drink whiskey.

... with wealth comes headaches. More people in upper income brackets buy headache remedies than those in lower income brackets.

... people in upper income brackets buy their beer in cans. People in lower income brackets buy their beer in bottles.

... more people in lower income brackets buy margarine.

... practically every Italian family in Rainier Valley has a fig tree.

PART III

In which we take you on
mouth-watering dining
adventures

RESTAURANTS

At the moment, I would be willing to risk a small wager that there is no city in the United States where you can get a better meal at a more reasonable price than in a Seattle restaurant. And there isn't a single one where you have to "buy" your table from the head waiter or where the price on the menu is not the price you find on the check, no matter how much you have to drink.

To me it is an astonishing fact that you can buy a good lunch in a good restaurant for as little as 96c. (The balance of your dollar is swallowed by our state government, which has a voracious tax appetite all of its own.)

It isn't necessary to dig very deep for the reason. Twelve years ago there wasn't a native who would openly admit we had a decent restaurant in town. Today, that same native is afraid there are too many top-flight restaurants. And in some respects he was right on both fronts.

Competition for the customer's dollar in Seattle is the keenest it has been in our history. There are more good restaurants per 1,000 population here than anywhere in the world. A strategic combination of decor, flavor, service, and price is essential to survival.

Twelve years ago our native did not realize that liberalization of our liquor laws had paved the way for the creation of some of the most sensitively-imaginative restaurants in the world. We're a well-traveled people and after a decade of comparison with other cosmopolitan cities, we are amazed at the imbecility of many national writers who mistake antiquity for quality and arbitrarily rule out any restaurant that didn't exist before the advent of modern refrigeration.

We're more knowledgeable than we were a few years ago. We've had a chance to compare the price-flavor-decor-service combo, and presently—with the federal government peering over our expense-account shoulders, we're extremely price conscious. And the restaurant that keeps price in mind gets the trade—if it also has the other factors.

We worry that we now have too many restaurants . . . and perhaps we should. Twenty per cent of the "mainline" restaurants in the first "Rainier", published seven years ago, no longer are in existence. On the other hand, many more than that have sprung up.

Many of us do not realize that most of the old restaurants went out of existence in favor of freeways and new buildings because we're the youngest big city in the United States . . . that while we have been enjoying a 20% increase in population, 12 of the top 20 cities in this country have lost population (most of them on the eastern seaboard as people move west).

We're a young city with young restaurants. And because we're young and new and vigorous, we have taken advantage of technological advances in facilities for preparing and serving food made possible by American ingenuity. We do not necessarily subscribe to the theory that a foreign accent is essential to a fine hand at the kitchen stove, although we have our share of chefs trained in the "old country".

In our highly competitive restaurant industry, business acumen is an essential concomitant of artistry. And the consumer benefits.

We are beginning to realize the high cost of household help is levelling the price between domestic and professional luxury dining. A housewife cannot prepare the kind of a meal she can purchase in a restaurant (often at a lower price) and also enjoy the company of her guests.

Our restaurants still are predominantly "charcoal broilers". It is sad but true that our competitive restaurateurs have recognized the average American's idea of a real gastronomic treat is limited to steak and prime ribs. And don't think this thought isn't shared by a few Frenchmen. You can't buy beef like ours in Europe which is probably why there aren't more charcoal broilers over there.

Being located where we are, we always have been partial to seafood and are connoisseurs. We recognize that unlike beef, any food taken from the sea starts losing flavor from the moment it is lifted out of salt water. Because it is economical to

124

boil seafood in oil we have been educated to enjoy deep-fried fish.

But competition is entering the picture and it is possible to find crab legs, oysters, sole, scallops, prepared delicately in wine and butter. Many of our restaurateurs have reached a high degree of perfection in the preparation of salmon—a delicacy that cannot be matched elsewhere in the world.

"Americanized" Chinese food, served in a lustreless atmosphere has been a regular feature of our dining-out diet ever since we stopped using coolie labor in the construction of our railroads 70 years ago. It is tasty, inexpensive, goes well with liquor and doesn't raise hell on the bath room scales the next morning.

Trader Vic introduced this same general kind of food under the more glamorous title of "Polynesian", which I am happy to state is a most flavorful addition to our gourmet dining.

Like the Chinese food, we've always had Japanese food served under the same dingy circumstances, but glamour was served with it when Mr. Seko introduced us to *Bush Garden* and now *Nikko* has followed along in the same tradition.

For some reason, we're absolutely ecstatic about Italian food, and I would imagine we have more Italian restaurants than any other except the ubiquitous charcoal broilers. Italian food goes with the generally relaxed, casual friendliness that goes with the kind of people who like living here.

There are more restaurants in the Puget Sound area than we will visit in our lifetime. It is entirely possible that you will have a "find" we haven't "found". On the other hand, we have made a conscientious effort to provide you with as wide as possible a choice in the establishments listed. And as new ones enter the scene, you will find them in our *Seattle Guide,* which comes out weekly and is available at most hotels, motels, restaurants, department stores and office buildings.

We believe you will enjoy dining in any or all of the following:

Adolfo's

Adolfo's is one of the reasons Seattle people are just crazy about Italian food. You'd never think a restaurant on Airport Way on the edge of our industrial district would rate as one of our "mainline" restaurants, but this one does.

It didn't appear in our last book and we got enough calls to cause us to try it out ourselves. We were not disappointed. The parking is easy, which is always handy. The decor is really quite simple.

It has the generally relaxed atmosphere of a neighborhood spot "run by the family" where everybody knows everybody else. But that isn't the drawing card that has made this place a Seattle Habit.

The flavor is great. That's what has done the trick. Raviolis made in their own kitchen . . . little attention to detail like imported provolone cheese for pizza topping—these are the things that please us and cause us to suggest it to you.

CHICKEN SAUTE' SEC (serves 4)

½ chicken, cut in 4 pcs.	½ c whole French
flour	mushrooms
butter and olive oil	touch chili pepper
1/4 c chicken bouillon.	salt—black pepper
½ green pepper, sliced	touch garlic salt
½ dry onion, sliced	½ c sherry
3 leaves rosemary	2 oz. fresh diced
	potatoes

Flour chicken. Braise in butter and oil until brown. Drain off most of oil; scrape pan with wine. Add vegetables, seasoning and chicken bouillon. Simmer 20 min. Serve with spaghetti.

3924 Airport Way
MA 2-1119
11 am-legal clsng
Cocktails
Dinner frm $2.50

Andy's Diner

Andy is a big boy who still loves to play with trains. His restaurant is made up of a series of railroad cars, vintage early 1900's, and the walls are decorated with pictures of old cars and locomotives, with legends describing them.

We're very fond of his ground sirloin of beef. It's processed in his own meat grinders, mixed with chopped bermuda onions, eggs, croutons and Andy's own herb seasoning, then broiled over charcoal. We also urge your attention to his hash browns, fried onion rings, apple or loganberry pies and big thick slices of egg bread. And he's a fine hand with steaks, too.

Andy has an ability to pick friendly waitresses (whom he refers to as sales girls) . . . a perceptive eye for choice cuts of meat . . . an absolute mania for cleanliness . . . and all in all, a talent for putting together a good organization that delivers good hearty food to you in a pleasant atmosphere.

2963 4th S.
MA 4-4097
11:30 am-9 pm
Cocktails
A la carte frm $2

GROUND SIRLOIN OF BEEF *(serves 5)*

2½ lb. grnd. sirloin steak	1½ t blk. pepper
1½ t Accent	1/4 t oregano
2 t salt	1/4 t thyme
1½ t Lawry's season. salt	½ med. onion, chop.
	½ c egg bread, chop

Combine all ingredients. Mold into 5 cakes, and broil or braise.

128

Bib 'N Tucker

Don't be fooled by the folksy name, this is an extremely smart dining spot that manages to make itself enticing to the younger generation as well as to their elders.

There is no other place in the world where you can find Quinault salmon as well prepared. And in case you don't know what Quinault salmon is, only Indians are permitted to sell it commercially from the Quinault River on the Olympic Peninsula. It is the only kind of salmon of this type in the world . . . rich, juicy, delicious.

There are menus for children, crayons to entertain them—plus a scale of prices that will be pleasing to a budget-minded father.

They take special pride in their rolls and baked desserts, which are made in their own kitchen. This, plus the special dishes developed in the Western Hotels experimental kitchens, makes the restaurant a favorite for family dining "out".

HAWAIIAN SHRIMP CURRY (serves 6)

1 qt scalded milk	*1½ T curry*
2 lb. fresh shrimp	*powder*
1 fresh grated cocoanut	*1½ T flour*
1 large onion sliced	*½ T cornstarch*
2 cloves garlic	*½ t brown sugar*

Scald milk. Add cocoanut, let stand. Saute onion and garlic in butter. Add milk and 1 cup chicken broth. Add curry and sugar. Simmer 20 min.—do not boil—stir constantly. Strain mixture through cheesecloth. Reheat and thicken with cornstarch and flour. Add shrimp, salt. Serve with steamed rice.

7th & Pine
MA 4-1400
6:30 am-10 pm
Cocktails
Entertainment
Dinners frm $2.35

129

Bob's Landing

Located right on Lake Washington, a little north of the Floating Bridge, this attractive restaurant neatly proves the point made by our previous book on Seattle restaurants: that we not only offer magnificent scenery, we offer fine dining to go with it.

Bob's big windows command a sweeping view of our beautiful lake. By day you get pretty-as-a-postcard views of sailboats, waterskiers and—when it chooses to reveal itself—our most famous piece of landscape, Mt. Rainier. At night you have a glamorous vista of lights twinkling across the lake, and along the famous floating bridge.

A top favorite here you might like to try is the combination plate of steak and lobster. Fish dishes are very popular, too, and there's a good array of steaks. The atmosphere of the place is relaxed and informal.

Weather permitting, you'll enjoy dining outside on the terrace, overlooking a veritable forest of sailboat masts.

HALIBUT POACHED IN WINE (serves 4)

3 lb. halibut	pinch tarragon, fennel,
1 c wine	and chervil
cream sauce	

100 Lakeside
EA 2-2175
11:30 am-10 pm
Open Sun.
Dinners frm $2.95

Poach in wine and herbs, covered, until fish flakes. Use stock for regular cream sauce and pour over fish. Add salt just before serving.

130

Bryan's Lake Terrace

Essentially a family dining spot, with outdoor dining when the weather is good. And if you're thinking of taking the children out for Sunday dinner, it would be a good idea to telephone ahead for reservations.

The roast leg of lamb, featured on Sunday only, attracts a lot of regular customers. And while you can count on a charcoal broiler, this is not the only attraction. You'll also find pan-fried chicken and chicken livers, Swiss steak with rolled potato pancakes, veal cutlets and prime ribs. And they are famous for their french fried jumbo Louisiana shrimp.

They also do their own rolls and are very proud of their cheesecake.

Special menu (and prices) for children. The surroundings are comfortable, the food flavorful and the prices generally moderate. Located across the boulevard from Green Lake.

CHEESE CAKE (serves 10-12)

1½ lbs. Philadelphia
    Cream Cheese
5 whole eggs
1 c granulated sugar
18 graham crackers,
    crushed

1½ t vanilla
1 T sugar
1 T butter
1½ pt. sour cream
½ c sugar
1½ t vanilla

Put cheese through ricer. Beat eggs into cheese, one at a time. Add 1 c sugar—1½ teaspoons vanilla. Cover bottom of round 8" baking pan with crackers mixed with 1 T butter and 1 T sugar. Pour batter over this carefully. Bake 300° 1 hour. Top cake with 1½ pt. commercially soured cream mixed with ½ c sugar and 1½ t vanilla. Bake 5 min.— cool—refrigerate.

7850 N Greenlake
LA 3-9529
5:30-9:30 pm
Sun. 1-8 pm
Wine & beer
Dinners frm $2.75

Bull 'N Bear

An entirely joyous restaurant to write about because unlimited imagination has been employed to make it suit our financiers—up to and including the fact that most of them are tighter than Swiss watches.

The menu is printed on a stock certificate, which should make most of the customers feel at home. You can get an inexpensive cup of soup if the stock market is down, but risk capital is engaged on a bet that you'll like the rarebeef, hot pastrami and corned beef sandwiches in that order, involving investments around $1.15-$1.20. There are hamburgers in 13 "nationalities," a "Greek" Goddess and other salads.

Even if you have no more artistic imagination than a stock broker, the dedicated perfection of the Bull'N Bear theme should get through to you—it even extends to the men's and ladies' rooms, which are decorated with $25,000 worth of *real* stock certificates.

GREEK GODDESS SALAD

Using individual dishes, make bed of lettuce. Add layer of sliced cooked potatoes, shredded lettuce, sprig of watercress. Place green pepper rings on top of watercress. Around the dish, place wedges of tomato, avocado, Feta cheese and sliced cucumbers. Place cooked beet slices on top of that and put one shrimp on top of each beet slice. Lay anchovy fillets on. Garnish with Greek olives, pieces of red sweet pepper and fancy-cut radishes, one whole green onion.

500 Union
MA 4-1646
7 a.m.-7:30 p.m.
Mon.-Fri.
Beer
Sandw. from 75c

Mix olive oil, wine vinegar, oregano, salt, pepper and pour on top.

Bush Garden

Japan has had an impact on many facets of Seattle living, and one of the nicest is this picturesque and authentic restaurant.

If you are unacquainted with Japanese food, abandon your concern, adjust your chopsticks and plunge in. The food is not only exotic and interesting, it is very palatable. Kimono-clad waitresses will cook sukiyaki right at your table, or introduce you to an Oriental approach to steak, and intrigue you with a series of unusual tidbits for side dishes.

Your party may occupy one of the shoji-screened tatami rooms, where you step out of your shoes and sit on the floor to dine. (A well under the table accommodates your legs comfortably.)

(After a 10-year success here, Bush Gardens have also been opened in Portland and San Francisco.)

MR. SEKO'S SUKIYAKI (serves 6)

2½ lbs. sukiyaki beef strips
suet as required
1 sm can bamboo shoots
4 bunches green onions, 1½" cuts
4 large onions, sliced
1 small can yam noodles
1 cake tofu (bean curd)
1 c soy sauce
2 c water
3 T sugar
½ c sake or wine

Sear meat in rendered suet - - push to one side of pan - - add vegetables, a serving at a time, in separate piles, with ½ cup sauce over (last 4 ingredients), uncovered, until vegetables are tender but crisp: add yam noodles-heat-serve with rice. (to each serving of veg. cooked, add ½ cup sauce—meat may be removed and added to each serving to reheat with tofu.)

614 Maynard
MU 2-6830
5 pm-legal clsng.
Cocktails
Dinners frm $3.50

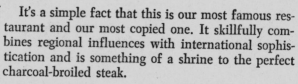

Canlis

It's a simple fact that this is our most famous restaurant and our most copied one. It skillfully combines regional influences with international sophistication and is something of a shrine to the perfect charcoal-broiled steak.

Poised on a hill overlooking Lake Union, the handsomely designed building features regional stones, timbers, and crafts, accented by nuances of Hawaii (where Canlis opened his original restaurant) and the Orient. To the rich yet subdued contemporary interior have been added the gracenotes of nisei waitresses in colorful kimonos.

You can get salmon, lobster, chicken, calves liver . . . but most of all you can get the New York steaks and the filet mignon by which most others are compared. Preceded at its best by the superb Canlis green salad and accompanied by a baked potato with special condiments.

CANLIS' SHRIMP (serves 8)

2 lbs. large shrimp in shell	½ t pepper
	2 oz. dry vermouth
1 oz. butter	½ lemon, juiced
1 oz. olive oil	½ t salt

Blend oil and butter in large skillet. Add shrimp, salt and pepper. (Be generous with salt in this dish). Cook until golden red and well done. Raise fire to very hot; add lemon juice and vermouth and cook one minute, stirring or shaking constantly. Serve as entree or appetizer.

2576 Aurora N.
AT 3-3313
5:30-11:30 pm
Cocktails
Entertainment
Dinners frm $3

134

Captain's Table

When Ivar Haglund, the restaurant genius, opened this restaurant there was some question about whether or not this city was mature enough to embrace it.

The Captain's Table is living proof that we not only have a "past" but an entirely elegant and colorful past . . . documented by pages from turn-of-the-century newspapers . . . brocaded elegance . . . chandeliered, statued, red and gold elegance.

Someone has said it's an atmosphere where a lady could be comfortable having the "vapors" but would postpone them to dine lustily on red snapper . . . clam bisque . . . prawns . . . oysters, all prepared with a degree of excellence that makes Ivar one of our most successful restaurant men.

It provides a pleasant Victorian nostalgia, if you happen to be that old . . . and beautifully satisfies that inner feeling of emptiness if you happen to be hungry.

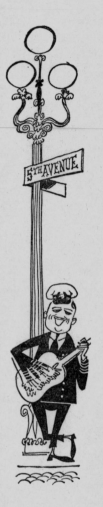

FERMIERE SAUCE (Good over sole or halibut)

4 T butter	1/4 c hot milk
1 c onion, chopped	1/4 c sauterne
1 c leeks, chopped	salt and pepper to taste
1 T flour	

Saute' onion and leeks in butter. Remove. Stir flour into pan butter, then milk. As it thickens, thin with wine. Season; return onion and leeks to sauce. (If fish juices are left from cooking, add to sauce but add more flour to thicken.)

1429 5th Ave
MA 2-7508
11 am-legal clsng
Cocktails
Ala Crt frm $1.95

Casa Villa

I keep running into interesting people I know here . . . the kind of people who respond to the warm, Italian friendliness of George DeJulio . . . who have a canny knowledge of good Italian food and enjoy the pastas, even if they *should* be on a diet.

A few minutes from downtown, the Casa is a villa-type building surrounded by easy parking. Inside the use of shutters, brick walls, Italian glass lanterns provides an atmosphere that seems to encourage friendly table-hopping in the older set and enhance the cause of true love for the younger set.

The menu is fairly hearty and predominantly Italian . . . offering spaghetti, ravioli and such, along with good salads and the more popular forms of meats. A bottle of good, red Italian wine would be a nice addition to your meal, too.

CHICKEN CACCIATORE (serves 4)

2½ lb. frying chicken (8 pcs.)	2 T parsley, chopped
1 small can mushrooms	½ c olive oil
4 T onions, diced	½ c sauterne
4 T grn. pepper diced	½ c chicken bouillon
1 tomato, diced	pinch salt, pepper,
1 clove garlic, minced	oregano

Sauté onions and garlic in oil. Remove. Sauté chicken lightly. Add wine—cook five minutes. Add bouillon and other ingredients. Bake 325° 25 min. Turn chicken while baking.

1823 Eastlake E
EA 3-7400
11 am-legal clsng
Cocktails
Entertainment
Dinners frm $2.50

Cascade Room

When we're looking around for a change of pace at lunch, we frequently select the Cascade Room in one of our leading department stores, The Bon Marche. It's easily approachable across the sky bridge from the parking garage, prices are reasonable . . . the food and drinks excellent.

And the lovely models who daily d i s p l a y the newest ideas in fashion detract nothing from the occasion.

However, getting back to food—you'll find homemade breads, very attractive salads, flavorful casseroles and luscious desserts, all prepared with meticulous care. Men customers go overwhelmingly for the ham and eggs Hawaiian.

The decor is spacious and comfortable, done in soft greens and browns and features motifs taken from Northwest Indian art.

BAKED DUNGENESS CRAB SALAD (serves 6-8)

3 c fresh Dungeness
  crabs
1 c blanched, slivered
  almonds
1 4-oz. can pimientos,
  cut in strips
1/4 c lemon juice
1½ c mayonnaise

1 med. sized onion,
  chopped fine
2 c diced parboiled
  celery, salt, paprika
1 c corn flakes,
  crumbled
½ c Tillamook
  cheese, grated

Mix all ingredients except corn flakes and cheese. Thin mayonnaise with lemon juice. Turn into shallow buttered casserole. Cover top with corn flakes, sprinkle with cheese. Bake 350°—25 min.

3rd & Pine
MA 4-1234
Mon 12-3; 5-8 pm
Tues-Sat-11-3 pm
Cocktails
Entertainment

Cloud Room

The Cloud Room, atop the Camlin Hotel, was one of the first restaurants to go up in the sky and give guests an opportunity to enjoy Seattle's surrounding seascape and landscape while dining. Now it has undergone refurbishing as the Camlin moves ahead with cabanas, swimming pool, and sun decks to bring country club living downtown.

A wonderful view of the city in luxurious surroundings close to the center of town . . . featuring onion pie with prime ribs . . . breast of chicken Cordon Bleu, Puget Sound salmon . . . even salmon kabobs on flaming sword . . . butterfly steak flambe' . . . Escoffier Sauce imported from England, sap sago cheese from Switzerland . . . and Coffee Camlin which has cocoanut syrup, 2 kinds of coffee plus rum, topped with coffee-seasoned whipped cream.

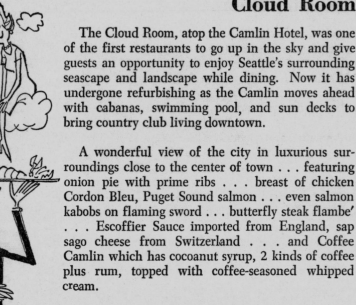

CRAB AND CHEESE SOUP *(serves 4)*

6 oz. Dungeness crab meat	½ c flour
	½ t MSG
½ oz. grated Romano cheese	1 cube butter
	1 qt cream
1/4 c sherry	1 qt fish bouillon
1/4 t dry mustard	dash Worcestershire
	salt and pepper

Melt butter until slightly brown, add crab meat and wine. Saute' until wine has evaporated. Add mustard and Worcestershire sauce. Blend in flour. Cook few minutes over slow fire. Add cream and fish bouillon slowly. Add cheese and MSG, salt and pepper. Simmer 5 minutes to cook raw flavor out of flour.

9th & Pine
MU 2-0100
12n-12m
Cocktails
Entertainment
Open Sun
Dinners frm $3.50

138

Crabapple

Periodically, we take the trek across the Lake Washington Floating Bridge for lunch or dinner at the Crabapple because we think it captures the spirit of stylish informality that personifies the best of our living here.

It's in the heart of Bellevue . . . features a stone fireplace . . . beechwood posts . . . enormous rough-hewn ceiling beams . . . and huge windows that make our outdoors a part of the inside scene.

We can count on the usual Clark Restaurant specialties like the crab legs broiled in wine and butter . . . clams, oysters, prime ribs . . . all very well prepared and served in the pleasant spirit of our sophisticated "suburbia" and at prices that do not necessitate our taking out a second mortgage on the old homestead when it comes time to pay the check.

MR. BELLEVUE SANDWICH (serves 4-6)

4 c white sauce	6 turkey slices, (white)
½ lb. cheddar cheese	6 toast slices
1 T dry mustard	3 asparagus spears
speck cayenne pepper	per serving
paprika	3 half slices bacon
	per serving

Place turkey slices over toast. Place 3 asparagus spears and 3 half slices bacon over each serving. Smother with hot white sauce mixed with cheese. Sprinkle with paprika. Lightly brown under broiler. Serve in individual gondolas with tossed salad.

Bellevue
GL 4-6344
11 am-legal clsng
Cocktails
Entertainment
Sun 5-9 pm
Dinners frm $3.25

139

Dublin House

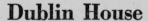

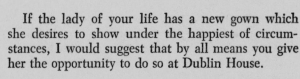

If the lady of your life has a new gown which she desires to show under the happiest of circumstances, I would suggest that by all means you give her the opportunity to do so at Dublin House.

Unlike many of our more elegant restaurants where secluded intimacy is stressed, the diners are "on stage" here. It's a high-ceilinged elegance to accommodate authentic and priceless memorabilia brought here from Dublin and London and arranged by Roland Terry.

A general feeling of "living" dark green pervades . . . intimacy is accomplished through eye-level lights and paintings . . . and a two-level table arrangement where people can see and be seen.

True to the tradition of the British Isles, prime ribs of beef is the favorite on the menu—food fit for an Irish Lord who should be so fortunate as to occupy such a skillfully arranged establishment.

BUNLAY STRIPS OF BEEF (serves 4-6)

1 lb. beef tenderloin	½ c sour cream
4 oz. unsalted butter	salt—pepper
4 shallots, chopped fine	1 t Escoffier Sauce Robert
2 oz. dry white wine	

Slice beef paper thin, two inches long. Melt butter to foaming, add meat and cook three minutes. Add salt, pepper and shallots. Toss: remove. In same pan, add wine, 1 teaspoon Escoffier sauce, ½ cup sour cream. Heat but do not boil. Pour over meat. Serve with rice, if desired. (Escoffier sauce can be substituted by Spanish sauce with touch of meat glace'.)

319 Union St
MA 3-7340
11 am-2 am
Cocktails
Entertainment
Dinners frm $3.25

140

El Gaucho

We haven't got a Madison Avenue, but we've got ad men like most—they've got an eye for smart, comfortable restaurants where the drinks and the steaks are good. So it's some sort of testimonial that you see a lot of ad men eating here.

In a setting flavored by South American motifs and extremely easy-to-observe waitresses, you can enjoy, if not a charcoal-broiled steak, then the flaming shish-kabob, lobster, salmon or lamb chops . . . good Caesar salads . . . and perhaps Cherries Jubilee or Cafe Diablo, a couple of worthwhile $2 investments.

Don't overlook the crab cocktail here, either—it's all big, succulent crablegs and outstanding.

Entrees are usually served with garlic bread, and baked potato topped with Gaucho cheese sauce and chopped onions.

SHISH KEBOB EL GAUCHO (serves 10)

6-8 lb. leg lamb trim-bone-cube 1½"	1½ t salt
½ c each oil - wine vinegar	2 t whl mint leaves
	1 small bay leaf
½ c burgundy	30 small onions (3 per serving)
1 t each of turmeric - garlic thyme-celery seed oregano-tarragon	10 whl. green tomatoes
	8 green peppers
	4 oz. 100 prf. vodka
	4 oz. brandy

Refrig. meat 24 hrs. in marinade above. Alternate meat with vegs. on a skewer. Broil over charcoal 15 or 20 min., turning. Dowse with liquor over HOT platter—ignite.

7th & Olive
MU 2-3202
11 am-legal clsng
Cocktails
Entertainment
Dinners frm $3.50

141

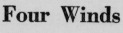

Four Winds

Four Winds is the only restaurant in town on a ship, the former *City of Everett,* which is living more elegantly on Lake Union than she ever did when she was plying the waters of Puget Sound as a ferryboat. Large view windows now look out on a downtown lake busy with seaplanes, yachts, workboats, and even a nearby submarine.

The decor and food take their theme from New Orleans and the likes of Jean LaFitte, who evidently must have thoroughly enjoyed a good steak and creole-type cooking. But I'll bet they never were treated to the delicacy of a Caesar salad like the one prepared temptingly and deliciously at your table here.

Very good food, and dancing, in an unusual setting which can be reached by car or boat.

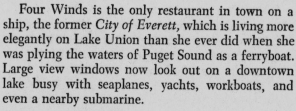

DEVILED CRAB AU GRATIN *(serves 6)*

2 c crab meat	bread crumbs
2 c white sauce	3/4 t chili
1/8 c grated Parmesan	powder
cheese	1/3 t salt
1/4 c sherry	1/4 t Accent
1/4 c dry white wine	pinch mace
1½ T prepared	dash Tabasco
mustard	

Wstlke N & Aloha
MA 3-4155
11:30 am-legal
clsng
Cocktails - dancing
Dinner frm $3.25

Mix all ingredients except crumbs in white sauce. Add crab meat. Fill shells. Sprinkle with bread crumbs and melted butter. Broil until crumbs brown.

Franco's Hidden Harbor

Recently a damp skindiver surprised the patrons here by flapping in on his flippers, sitting down at the bar, raising his visor and ordering a drink. He was the plumber! . . . and he'd just finished a job under water for the restaurant, which is located at lake level right in the middle of one of our covered yacht moorages.

This is a most interesting restaurant for visitors, as you dine on the level of the yachts which are gently riding at anchor all about you. In addition you can dine outside on the dock any time of year, because infra-red lights keep you warm out there.

Appropriately enough, the menu pays its respect to marine foods . . . and you should particularly consider the saute'ed Dungeness crab legs, tiny pan-fried Quilcene oysters and broiled lobster tails.

A smartly designed restaurant that's smart enough to make the most of our wonderful water-borne assets.

NELSON DUNGENESS CRAB LEGS (serves 4)

1½ lb. Nelson's fresh
   Dungeness crab legs
1½ green peppers
½ dry onion
2 hearts of celery
1 bunch green onions

2½ oz. sauterne
1/8 lb. butter
1/8 t thyme
½ t salt
1/4 t black
   pepper

Saute' diced vegetables in butter five minutes. Add crab legs. Saute' the mixture additional five minutes. Add wine, salt, pepper and thyme. Cover pan and saute' over slow fire for about 10 minutes. Franco suggests you serve en casserole.

1500 Westlake N
AT 2-0501
11 am-legal clsng
Cocktails
Dinners frm $2.75

143

Frederick and Nelson

Nobody other than a Seattle native would understand the lengths Frederick and Nelson goes to for perfection in preparation of their tearoom food.

For years and years they have been paying premium prices to get uniform size and quality in fruits and vegetables—one reason their salad assortments are so attractive and tasteful. They have bought chicken and eggs from the same source for almost 40 years and built a reputation for their creamed chicken. They make their hand-made bread from unbleached flour, virtually non-existent these days. And their own ice cream plant produces their notable ice creams and famous Frango dessert.

The tea room has been pleasing Seattle women and their daughters for years . . . and now they permit men in their own sanctuary, the Men's Grill, and have a buffet service, too, for the hurried shopper. A nearby department also sells dining delicacies that you can take home.

CRAB RAVESSANT

A salad distinguished for its piquant combination of flavors. On each individual plate (generous dinner size) place a base of lettuce. On this alternate grapefruit segments, slices of avocado and extra-large legs of our superlative native Dungeness crab, placing them in a beautiful fan shape. With this, Frederick's serves their Chiffonade Dressing, a blending of mayonnaise, chili sauce, tomato catsup, pickle relish and chopped olives. (similar to a 1000 Island dressing.) In fact, you can buy the Chiffonade dressing in Frederick's Delicacy Shop.

Fifth & Pine
MU 2-5500
Mon 12-3;
5:30-7:30 pm
Tues-Sat
11:30-2:30
Tea 2:30-4:30

144

French Quarter

There are bound to be those who will be a bit confused by the fact that the French Quarter does not serve French food. But who needs it when the drinks you do get are served by statuesque Parisian bar girls in somewhat scanty costumes?

At the time this is being written, the management is thinking of restoring snails to the menu because of popular demand. But beyond that, they stick to their highly popular steaks and their noon-time feature, the 96c lunch, served in an atmosphere of French posters, brick, and dark stained wood.

For the monster appetite, they serve a 2 lb. T-bone at $3.75 . . . other key favorites are their New York steak, tenderloin beef kabobs, and chicken pot pie. At noon 96c gets you an entree plus salad and bread or plus soup and salad. For cocktail hour there's the Downbeat Room, with its motif of musical instruments.

SAUTE'ED TRIPE (serves 4)

2 lbs. tripe, 2" squares   ½ garlic clove
1½ stalks celery, cut   2/3 c butter
1/4 c parsley, chopped   2/3 c bread crumbs
1/4 t thyme   ½ T salt
½ lrg. onion, sliced   8 peppercorns, cracked
                              1 T chives, chopped

Cover tripe with cold water; add seasonings, celery and parsley. Bring to boil. Cover; lower heat. Simmer 4 hrs. Let stand in broth until cold. Drain, dip in melted butter and bread crumbs. Saute' in remaining butter until golden brown. Top with chives.

1326 7th Ave
MU 2-8474
11 am-legal clsng
Cocktails
Dinners frm $2.25

Golden Lion

One of my favorite Kipling quotes could have come from here because the waiters are dressed in "more than Oriental splendor" . . . and they are right at home in a background of custom-painted red and gold fabric accented by burnished walnut paneling befitting Queen Victoria's India.

Featuring dramatic dining, their 7 delectable dishes served on a flaming sword are preceded by the resonant boom of a huge East Indian gong and lowered lights. Specialties also include chafing dishes like baby lobster tails bathed in mushrooms, cream and spices set aflame in brandy . . . broiler, skillet, and oven dishes . . . flaming desserts, all presented with a flair.

Their "Champagne Dinner" with breast of guinea hen under glass, prime rib or baked ham, is the talk of the town.

ROCK LOBSTER TAILS EN BROCHETTE

Marinate lobster for 2 hours in:

2½ c olive oil	1 T maggi
1 grated onion	1 T Trader Vic glacé
1 T chili powder	1 clove chopped garlic
1 T coriander	1 T lemon juice
1 T ginger	1 c sherry
1 T curry powder	1 c sauterne
1 oz salt	1 c chopped parsley

Olympic Hotel
MU 2-7700
Mon-Fri 12n-12m
Sat 5 pm-12m
Cocktails
Entertainment
Dinners frm $3.75

Wrap 1 inch cube fresh pineapple in hickory-smoked bacon. Around this, roll marinated lobster tail. Put on skewer and broil.

Grove

So-named because the background gives the impression that you are in a grove of trees, the Grove features steaks, lamb chops, spare ribs, calf's liver . . . and fresh king salmon from the charcoal broiler when it is in season . . .

And may we recommend the latter if you're sampling our salmon. Owner Les Brainard has his own special seasoning and you will enjoy the "seafood that made Seattle famous" as it is prepared under his direction.

From the open hearth come prime ribs of beef au jus . . . chicken in the pot (like grandma used to prepare it, except the pot is silver) . . . boiled beef in the pot . . . and imported lobster thermidore en shell as the Friday special.

If you enjoy good meat, well-selected and well-prepared, which most Americans do, you'll go home— wherever "home" is—with a wonderful memory after dining here.

BOILED BEEF IN POT *(serves 16-18)*

1 *choice brisket, 14 lb.*	1 T *celery salt*
water to cover	1 T *Accent*
1 c *onion powder*	12 *carrots*
1 T *garlic powder*	25 *small onions*
8 *bay leaves*	20 *small potatoes*
3 T *whole pepper-corn*	*meat glaze*
½ c *salt*	18 oz. *noodles*

Soak meat overnight in first 7 ingredients. Simmer until fork tender, about 4 hrs. Cook vegs. and noodles separately in same water: Serve in silver casserole in layers (noodles, sliced meat, vegs.) Pour over sauce of stock and meat glaze.

Harold's Satellite

Although the freeway dispossessed Harold Frye from his longtime location on Eastlake, he has advantageously moved his building a few blocks north and landed on a Lake Union dock, with a spectacular view of the sunset through the Lake Washington Ship Canal.

As his new name indicates, he's featuring the space age in his decor—including a galaxy in the ceiling of the Galaxy Room.

He still gets his corned beef from our favorite corned beef provender, Jimmy Akrish. Also features a spencer roast, which we guessed correctly was the eye of the prime rib . . . cold, firm, tasty salmon from Bristol Bay . . . South African lobster tails, charcoal broiled.

It's the same genial Harold in the same building with the addition of a huge sun-deck for outdoor dining, and parking spots for 36 yachts if you don't happen to own a car.

ROQUEFORT CHEESE DRESSING

3 cups mayonnaise   *juice of two lemons*
4 oz. grated Roquefort
  cheese

2501 Fairview E.
EA 5-6100
12n-legal clsng
Cocktails
Sun 1-8 pm
Dinners frm $3

Mix well by hand or electric mixer. Especially good on tossed green salad.

148

Hilton Inn

Garden Terrace, the posh restaurant at the new Hilton Inn, is a pleasing example of an emerging Northwest architecture . . . utilizing full-length windows to make the outdoor scene a part of the interior decor.

Golds, greens and browns highlight original paintings by Northwest artists and two-story windows focus on the outdoor garden courtyard, pool, native trees and rhododendron collection.

Operated by Peter Canlis of Honolulu and Seattle fame, the menu features such things as fresh Dungeness Crab leg fingers with mustard and mayonnaise . . . Quilcene oysters on the half shell with cocktail sauce . . . fruit salad Hawaiiana . . . beef a la Stroganoff . . . avocado stuffed with crab or shrimp—

And, of course, steaks (ham or beef) and lamb chops selected and prepared with the perfection that is the basis of Canlis' success.

CANLIS' FRENCH DRESSING

1 c olive oil	1/4 t salt, 1 clove garlic
1 c red wine vinegar	1/4 t fresh mint, chopped
1/4 t fresh ground pepper	1/4 t oregano

Place all ingredients into a bottle and allow to stand, then shake vigorously and serve.

Hiway 99 & Airprt
CH 4-4800
11:30 am-lgl clsng
Cocktails
Entertainment
Sun 3-10 pm
Dinners frm $3.95

Hofbrau

If you're in the mood for young, noisy gaiety and excellent German food, especially the sandwiches, then this is just your stein of beer.

A separate building that reminds me of a Hansel and Gretel cottage, it is a modernized version of a German beer garden. And I will never forget the slightly befuddled lady who mistook the "Herren" (Men) for "Hers." (And I'll bet she will never forget it, either!)

Neither will I ever forget the nicely off-shoulder blouses of the waitresses. The management opines the three most favorite foods are German beefsteak . . . club steak . . . sauerbraten—in that order.

And the world's best beers are at your beck and call here under the happiest of circumstances.

GERMAN BREAD DUMPLINGS (serves 4)

1 lg loaf day-old wht bread
2 c flour
1 1/3 T salt
2 2/3 T poultry seasoning
3 lg (or 4 sm) eggs, beaten
1 1/3 milk
½ onion, chopped
2 T parsley, minced
½ lb. bacon, diced chicken base

Cube bread small and add flour, salt, poultry seasoning, onion and parsley. Cook bacon until crisp and leave in pan with fat. Beat eggs and milk together and add to very hot bacon and fat. Pour immediately on bread mixture, mix lightly to hold and let stand ½ hr. Drop by spoonful in boiling chicken stock and cook 8 min.

Hong Kong

No matter which way you slice your barbecued pork or chop your chop suey this is the most frequented Chinese restaurant in our International Settlement.

The name Hong Kong is no idle gesture. Sam Yee, the owner, and his two top chefs hail from that international city. The cooking is Cantonese . . . the sesame chicken boned, which I think is an important criterion. The food is clean, crisp and tasty.

This is very much a family restaurant, especially on Sunday. The kids get a great kick out of the aquarium that surrounds one of the supporting posts. Fathers enjoy the fact there is convenient parking in back.

If you like Chinese food prepared in the traditional manner we Americans have become accustomed to, you will find it done in a superior fashion here.

SUB-GUM ALMOND CHICKEN CHOP SUEY
(serves 4)

1 lb. chicken, diced
1 lb. lean pork, diced
1 can bamboo shoots, diced
1 can water chestnuts
1½ c celery, diced
1 c fresh mushrooms
½ c Chinese almonds
soy sauce, peanut oil

Fry chicken and pork in oil. In separate pan, cook bamboo shoots, water chestnuts, celery, mushrooms lightly in oil. Blanch almonds in oil in another pan. Turn meats, vegetables, and almonds into a bowl, add a little water, season with soy sauce and mix thoroughly. Sprinkle top with crushed blanched almonds and serve.

507 Maynard Ave
MA 2-0366
11:30 am-lgl clsng
Cocktails
Open Sun.
Dinners frm $2.25

151

Hyatt House

Spectacular new resort-type motel near the Seattle-Tacoma Airport with a dining room that makes you think of Grand Hotel . . . economically-sound on such a lavish scale because ours is the third largest "overseas" airport in the nation.

Enticing to the local trade because of a luxury weekend package permitting two to "get away from it all" for $29.50 . . . we like the bellboys in the Philip Morris outfits and the fact we can have lunch around the pool.

The menu is fantastically cosmopolitan, featuring such delicacies as breast of capon a la Kiev . . . roast Long Island duckling Bigarde, orange sauce . . . shashlik of choice lamb mignons.

You would scarcely expect something so plush near *our* airport—but there it is.

SMOTHERED VEAL CUTLET GENTILHOMME
(serves 8)

8 *veal cutlets, 5 oz. ea.*   *salt-pepper to taste*
flour, salt and pepper   *3 c thick cream sauce*
6 eggs, whipped   *1 c American cheese*
1 c onions, chopped   *few grns. cayenne*
3 lg. cloves garlic, minced *1/4 c butter*
2 c fresh tomato, diced   *2 in. slices avocado per*
1 T sugar   *serving of meat*

170th & Hwy 99 S
CH 4-6000
Mon-Fri
11 am-12m
Sat 5 pm-12m
Cocktails
Entertainment
Sun 3-11 pm
Dinners frm $3.50

Dredge veal in seasoned flr., then egg. Saute' in butter, place on baking pan; top ea. with Portugaise sauce; (Saute' onions in butter, add garlic, tomato, sugar, salt and pepper). Lay avocado over ea.; top with Mornay sauce (crm. sauce, Amer. cheese, cayenne, butter). 4 T Parmesan cheese over all. Bake 450°, golden brown.

Ivar's Acres of Clams

Ivar's, located on one of our downtown piers, is a happily cluttered, rollicking institution, which is the product of Ivar's unlimited imagination and sense of humor.

He has embellished this restaurant with funny signs, masses of aquatic type gear, gimmicks for children, and his clientele includes absolutely everybody. He likes to think of this restaurant as the place where clams and culture meet.

While clam nectar and steamed clams are the heart of the place, you will find all manner of other foods enthusiastically dished up here, along with French fries, cole slaw and other suitable accompaniments.

There's a Fish Bar on the street, too, where you can get snacks and sit outside on Ivar's benches near the bright red firehouse or stroll along the waterfront. And you can rest assured that the seafood is always really fresh.

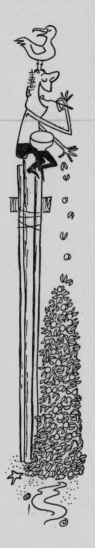

FILLETS OF SOLE MORNAY (serves 6)

2 c cream sauce	½ c parmesan cheese
1/3 c white wine	salt, white pepper, MSG
1/3 c melted butter	6 fillets of sole
2 egg yolks, beaten	

To cream sauce, add wine, butter, egg yolks, cheese, and seasonings. Place sole in shallow earthenware or Pyrex dish, pour small amount of melted butter and white wine over them, and bake in med. oven for about 6 min. Pour sauce over sole and put under the broiler until golden brown. Serve. (The chef suggests a bottle of Chablis or Riesling would be a happy addition to the meal.)

Pier 54
MA 4-6852
11 am-legal clsng
Cocktails
Open Sun
Dinners frm $1.95

153

Johnny's Dock

It is a terrible confession for me to make but Johnny's Dock is, uh, in, uh, *Tacoma*—but really not far into Tacoma, *quite* close to Seattle . . . and so extremely successful that a lot of Seattle people must be sneaking over there to eat.

I love a place like Johnny's Dock . . . right out at the end of pier 3 . . . past the warehouses and the industrial district—into contemporary luxury and food served by a guy who can't do anything except on a lavish scale.

It's a jutting-out building with a fly-away roof . . . all chocolate and yellow . . . with great beams and enormous windows overlooking Commencement Bay. Johnny Meaker says his three most favored items are steak, salmon—both charcoal broiled—and prawns—all done to perfection, like everything else here.

But if you have the kids, don't overlook Johnny's great weakness—great big, goopy, whipped cream packed sundaes.

POACHED SALMON AU RIESLING

2 qts. *water*	½ *sliced carrot*
1 2-inch *sliced onion*	6 *crushed peppercorns*
1 T *salt*	*sprig parsley, thyme,*
1 *bay leaf*	*celery*
1 *cup riesling*	

Bring to a boil, simmer 20 minutes. Cool slightly. Lower six 12-oz. fillets of salmon on a rack. Simmer salmon gently 25 minutes or until it flakes easily. Remove from liquid. Serve on hot platter. Garnish with lemon wedges, sliced cucumbers, parsley. Serve with hollandaise sauce.

Pier 3-Tacoma
BR 2-6789
11 am-legal clsng
Cocktails
Sun 2 pm-10 pm
Dinners frm $2.75

154

Kalua Room

When you walk into this South Seas atmosphere you can feel an instant lightening of the cares of the day. The Gwynne Austins, who have developed this delightful mirage, have incorporated their own spirit of adventure into the decor. Many of the authentic items you see have been personally collected in such places as Tahiti, to say nothing of under the sea where the Austins were the very divers who brought up some of the decorative shells.

There's a South Seas charm to the food, too. Chicken Kamaaina, for instance, which is boned and stuffed with fresh cocoanut and pineapple, and served with fried bananas . . . Teriyaki steak marinated in soy, ginger and garlic . . . prawns curry Samoa.

All this becomes even more delightful preceded by mysterious rum drinks served in exotic pottery and glassware.

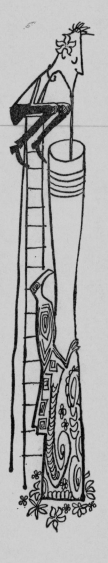

CHICKEN KAMAAINA (serves 4)

2 chickens, halved and boned	1/4 c melted butter
	1/3 c flour
12 pineapple spears	2 c hot milk
4 t shredded coconut	1/3 c pineapple juice
1 egg, beaten	MSG, salt, pepper
fine bread crumbs	1 T chicken base

Wrap ea. ½ chick. around 3 pineapple spears, 1 t coconut. Bake uncovered, ½ hr.-foil covered 15 min. Roll in egg and crumbs—saute' in oil. Add to pineapple sauce: blend butter, flr., hot milk, seasoning, chick. base. Serve with rice. Garnish with browned macaroon coconut, pimento.

6th & Union
MA 3-2920
6:30 am-lgl clsng
Cocktails
Dinners frm $2.75

155

King Oscar's

Seattle has the highest percentage in the United States of Scandinavians born in the "old country" and you'd think we'd have a dozen or more "houses" like this. It isn't that others haven't appeared on the scene. They have. But they've been up against a determinedly discriminating type of taste testers . . . and only King Oscar's has passed the taste test over the past quarter of a century.

Without question, Bill Jensen sets one of the finest Swedish Smorgasbords in the country. If you're of a mind to select an entree, may I recommend the Swedish pancakes filled with wine and cream sauce and served with chicken and mushrooms.

Located in one of our old mansions, this restaurant offers an unsurpassed view of the city and "the" mountain. About ten minutes from downtown, but never mind the time, gourmets have come from every corner of the earth for the privilege of sighing in ecstatic completeness at the end of a meal here.

BAVARIAN CHICKEN EN CASSEROLE

(serves 6)

6 *chicken breasts*	1/4 *c chicken broth*
½ *c butter*	½ *c white wine*
1/4 *t thyme*	12 *slices ham, cooked*
salt; ground pepper	½ *c light cream*
1 *T dehyd. chop. onion*	1 *t parsley flakes*

Shake chicken in flr. with salt, pepper and thyme. Saute' breasts in butter until brown. Add onion, broth and wine. Simmer, covered, 30 min. Stuff ham slices into slits cut at ea. side of breasts. Stir cream and parsley into broth and pour over chicken in individual casseroles. Bake 10 min. at 350°.

4312 Aurora N
ME 2-4992
Mon-Sat 5pm-12m
Cocktails
Sun 4-10 pm
Dinners frm $3

Lakewood Terrace

If the Northwest *has* country estate, riding to the hounds, country club type living, it's in the lake district just south of Tacoma. And created to serve this set is the Lakewood Terrace, in Lakewood Center—a "Williamsburg-y" styled shopping community.

It comes as a delightful surprise to find a continental menu and service housed in Northwest atmosphere of flagged foyer, driftwood stained natural wood areas, well-done candlelight colors and lighting. But the purpose of the design is borne out in the popularity among the residents for whom it was created—they love it and populate it regularly.

Olav Carlsen, the Danish maitre d' blends the Northwest and Europe happily in the food line. Especially tempting dishes are duck a la Bigarde flambe . . . tournedos de beouf Rossini . . . crepe Suzette.

Genuinely continental dining and good.

COCOTTE DE POULETTE AU VIN
(serves 4)

2 1/4 lb. spring chicken, **pinch garlic salt, paprika,**
    boned   **sweet basil**
onion, small amt., chopped **1 t salt**
1 c claret   **1/4 c butter**
1 T fresh parsley,   **pearl onions**
    chopped   **kabob mushrooms, whole**

Shake chicken with flour, salt, herbs. In heavy skillet, saute' pearl onions and mushrooms. Remove from pan and saute' chicken with chopped onion until golden. Add wine—simmer, covered, until tender. Strain the sauce over chicken in casserole: add mushrooms, onions and sprinkle with parsley.

6114 Motor Ave
SW Tacoma
JU 8-5215
8 am-legal clsng
Cocktails
Entertainment
wknd
Dinners frm $2.50

157

Legend Room

The Legend Room is part of the suburban branch of one of our fine department stores, the Bon Marche . . . located in America's first-of-its-kind suburban shopping center, Northgate. The food is so good that people eat there even when the shopping center is not open.

Thursday night's western buffet is a great family favorite which features Northwest foods . . . Tuesday noons feature fashion shows . . . any time is a good time to entice children with their own special menu and Tuesday and Saturday two people can have dinner for one price, $3.95.

The serene and spacious dining room and cocktail lounge are done in restful greens warmed with Northwest Indian motifs in rich colors. Foods, too, reflect the Northwest, with thoughtful treatment of clams, crab, salmon and beef, and beautiful salad concoctions featuring local fruits and vegetables.

BROILED SCALLOPS AND MUSHROOMS EN BROCHETTE (serves 2)

1 c cracker meal	1 t salt
1 t parsley chopped	8 scallops
1 t chives chopped	6 mushrooms
1 t marjoram	

Dip washed and dried scallops in melted butter. Roll in fine cracker meal that has been seasoned in herbs. String 4 scallops on each skewer, alternating with 3 saute'ed mushroom caps, uniform size. Broil until lightly browned on all sides. Serve with lemon parsley butter.

Northgate Mall
EM 2-1234
12n-10 pm
Cocktails
Dinners frm $2.70

158

Nikko

Food fit for a king . . . and certainly an Emperor
. . . as the chef here formerly served in the same
capacity to the Royal Family of Japan, and prepared
food for the Prince and Princess on their recent royal
visit here.

You'll probably think of ordering the niku or tori
sukiyaki . . . but do experiment with some side
dishes. Salmon sakamushi is tender and succulent,
the Nikko approach to lobster is most interesting,
and there's trout, crab and abalone enhanced by
mysterious sauces. The sashimi (sliced raw tuna
fish) doesn't really taste raw at all. Where beef or
steak is used, it is always choice, tender cuts.

Nikko is named after a city about 90 miles from
Tokyo and much of the authentic flavor of the
Japanese scene has been carefully recreated. To further the mood, sit-on-the-floor tatami rooms are
available to parties of 3 or more.

SALMON SAKAMUSHI (serves 6)

12 (3-oz.) slices salmon   6 T sake
6 slices lemon   dash aji-no-moto (MSG)
   (1/8" thick)   1 lemon, juiced
6 pieces konbu (sea-   equal amt. soy sauce
   weed) 1" sq.

Salt salmon. Stack. Let stand 3 or 4 min. Place 1
piece of konbu in individual saucer. Place 2 slices
salmon on top, overlapping each other, inserting
lemon slice between. Sprinkle 1 T sake over evenly.
In steamer, cook salmon on its saucer 7 to 10 min.
Serve with hot lemon soy sauce (last 3 ingredients.)

1306 King
EA 2-4641
5 pm-10 pm
Cocktails
Dinners frm $3.75

159

Nisco's

Here's a small jewel of intimately-lighted comfort designed to show your best girl off at her best and at the same time provide a surprisingly robust meal leaning toward steaks and veal scaloppine.

I don't know about the women of yesteryear, but I have found the present-day version is not the type to faint at the sight of a well-laden plate. Nick Nisco has dinners at various prices, but if you feel like shooting the works the "Salute to Century 21" is worth shooting for at $21. It involves leisurely dining for two with cocktails from the bar, antipasto, chateaubriand, cabernet, dessert, coffee and your favorite after-dinner drink.

As yet undiscovered by many in Seattle, but in my opinion destined for greatness because it subtly enhances a woman's beauty and unobtrusively satisfies the "inner woman."

VEAL SCALOPPINE (serves 4)

5th & Spring
MA 4-2944
Mon-Fri
11:30 am-2 am
Sat 4 pm-12m
Entertainment
Cocktails
Dinners frm $3.75

1½ lbs. veal (top round) cut 1/4 in. thick, 2 in. sq.
3/4 c diced onions
½ c fresh cut mushrooms

1 c diced green peppers
3 T Worcestershire sc.
1 t Accent
1 c sauterne
salt, pepper

Flour veal. Brown quickly in 3 T hot oil. Add vegetables. Add liquids. Simmer 15 min.

160

Norselander

The Norselander automatically is recognized as one of our leading seafood restaurants. Located on the west side of Queen Anne Hill, it has a commanding view of Puget Sound and the Olympic mountains—when they have a mind to display themselves.

It occupies the top floor of the Norway Center building that not only is a center for the activities of our Scandivanian community but contains the only commercial Kosher kitchen I know of in Seattle.

You would do well to order any seafood that fits your fancy. And if you have an appreciation of Norwegian fish cakes, here is the only place in town that serves them, to the best of my recollection.

A very colorful spot with a marine motif—and you try and figure out how they have both fish and birds in the same "aquarium." Also one of the few places where you can dance.

LOBSTER THERMIDOR (serves 2)

1 lobster (1½ or 2 lb.)	½ c sliced mushrooms
2 c white sauce	pinch cayenne
2 T dry sherry	bread crumbs, fine
1/8 t dry mustard	1/4 c parmesan cheese

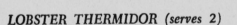

Remove stomach from lobsters, split lengthwise. Remove meat, cut into ½ inch pieces. Place shell in warm oven. Add mushrooms, saute'ed in butter, to white sauce along with seasonings, wine and lobster. Add to shells, sprinkle with cheese and bread crumbs. Drizzle melted butter over top. Brown under broiler.

300 3rd W
AT 4-8240
11:30 am-lgl clsng
Cocktails
Entertainment
Sun 3 pm-10 pm
Dinners frm $3

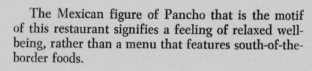

Pancho's

The Mexican figure of Pancho that is the motif of this restaurant signifies a feeling of relaxed well-being, rather than a menu that features south-of-the-border foods.

As a matter of fact, Pancho's is one of our pioneer open-pit restaurants starring charcoal broiled meats —and they do this so well you wind up feeling just like Pancho. You can even select your own steak and see the chef broil it to perfection. Other good ideas are double thick lamb chops . . . or flaming shish kabobs, beef brochette, or Stroganoff. Crisp green salads, good baked Idahos, and Pancho's special bread are other features.

The decor is in a smart Mexican motif . . . with each area arranged as a small, intimate dining spot that makes for a cozy informal feeling. Nice for luncheon, as well as dinners, and handily located downtown.

BEEF STROGANOFF (serves 4)

1/4 c beef gravy	2 T mushrooms, sliced
3/4 c sour cream	2 T sherry
6 thin slices beef	4 T butter
tenderloin	2½ c water
1 T green onion,	1 c wild rice
chopped	1 t salt

Boil salted water, add rice and return to a boil. Stir, cover and simmer twenty-twenty five minutes without lifting lid. Saute' beef in butter with onion and mushrooms. Add sherry, beef gravy and sour cream, mixed. Serve Stroganoff over the hot rice.

4th & Stewart
MU 2-1417
11 am-legal clsng
Cocktails
Dinners frm $3

162

Polynesia

C'est Impossible to go wrong on a "Tamaaraa" by George Olsen here. (As a starter, I'd try calling it a "Tam-ah-ah-ra-ah-ah.) In Sweden, you'd be asking for a private Smorgasbord for your table. In Hawaii, it would be a Luau. But it's a Tamaaraa in Tahiti. And when you enter the Polynesia, to all practical purposes, you have just arrived in Tahiti.

I suggest at least a party of six for your Tamaaraa because it comes in on a laden board borne by two men. Your wine is poured into graceful glasses from a beaten-up old teakettle because that's the custom in Tahiti.

Steaks and chops are under the heading: "Reminiscence of the United States." Saute'ed chicken livers and other French cooking is headed, "Memoirs From France."

A triple-peaked Polynesian longhouse on the end of a pier—with excellent food.

CHICKEN WRAPPED IN PAPER *(serves 6)*

2 t *prune sauce*
   (Chinese store)
2 t *bean sauce*
   (Chinese store)

1 *breast chicken, sliced*
   and cut in squares
1 t *MSG*
1 t *wht. wine*

Marinate one half hour. Deep fat fry, wrapped in foil, 3 min. (serve with picks as hors d'oeuvres.)

Pier 51
MA 4-6995
11 am-1 am
Cocktails
Entertainment
Dinners frm $3.65

Red Carpet

The pleasant connotations of "rolling out the red carpet" make up the theme here. The designers had an Old English motif in mind when they created the Red Carpet, but that's the only thing "old." This is one of our smartest restaurants . . . warmed by charming lamps . . . mellow bricks . . . stained wood . . . and a series of intimate nooks and crannies that permit you to dine in secluded elegance.

Located on the Westlake Mall, it's in the heart of our uptown shopping area and is identified by the gaslight torch near the entrance.

Featured foods include veal a la Oscar . . . New York steak and broiled scallops. I do go there because I dine well, but the fact it is patronized by some of the best-dressed women in the world is no deterrent whatsoever.

5th & Olive
MA 3-5226
11 am-legal clsng
Cocktails
Entertainment
Dinners frm $3.35

ROQUEFORT CHEESE CREAM DRESSING
(serves 8)

1½ lb grated Roquefort cheese
1 pt mayonnaise
1 c buttermilk
½ T Lawry salt

1 T Worcestershire sauce
juice of half lemon
dash Tabasco sauce

Mix well by hand or electric mixer

164

Roma

If I could do it, I would have a law passed requiring every citizen over 21 to pay a periodic visit to the Roma. That way three-quarters of the things we think bother us would be eliminated under the impact of simply dandy Italian food and a genial atmosphere where unhappiness is simply not permitted.

While still in our "skidroad" area downtown, they've gone and gotten all dolled up recently in a lot of Italian elegance. Nonetheless, Bill Gasperetti forgets he shouldn't meet you in shirtsleeves and brother John, who presides over the excellent kitchen, persists in the opinion that his brother has such a good time greeting people he isn't really working . . . which John considers a *bad* thing.

Raviolis, gnocchi and other forms of pasta are made in their kitchen, and for a change try spaghetti tossed with olive oil, butter and herbs. Other good bets are their treatment of rabbit, and their braised short ribs.

PESTO ALA GENOVESE *(serves 4)*

½ c fresh chopped parsley	½ c olive oil
1/4 c fresh grated parmesan cheese	2 T sweet basil
	2 pats butter, melted
	2 cloves garlic, minced

Mix ingredients in bowl. Pour over cooked spaghetti, macaroni, or gnocchi. Serve with additional grated cheese on top. This is a "green" sauce for pasta—which the Gasperettis suggest will make a newly interesting dish out of spaghetti and be a pleasant change from the usual tomato and meat type of sauce.

4th & Main
MA 3-5932
12n-legal clsng
Cocktails
Open Sun
Dinners frm $2.50

Rosellini's Four-10

Exuberant Victor Rosellini's Four-10 is a first port-of-call for gourmets on the swing through Seattle.

The cuisine and atmosphere is genuinely continental. The chef is a master of classic cookery and the waiters are at ease serving the most discerning and demanding diners.

You dine in a quietly elegant setting of rich, deep red played against black and embellished with touches of gold and white. Both the mood and the food are plush and sumptuous. Chicken Kiev and tortellini a la Romano are stars among the entrees.

Off the foyer, the Boulevard Room, with its gas-lit lamps and European cafe atmosphere, offers bright entertainment and cocktails.

We use this restaurant when we want to show visiting VIP's that Seattle offers posh dining to match Manhattan's celebrated spots.

410 University
MA 4-5464
11 am-legal clsng
Cocktails
Entertainment
Dinners frm $4.35

CHICKEN DORE, KIEV (serves 6)

6 chicken breasts, boned
12 oz. butter (2 oz. per breast)
flour
whole egg, stir with fork
bread crumbs
6 toast rounds

Roll flattened breasts around butter. Bread in flour, then beaten egg and lastly, crumbs. Saute' in butter until brown. Bake 450° 15 min. Serve on toast rounds. Pierce chicken so juices run onto toast.

166

Ruby Chow's

More on the sophisticated side than many of our Chinese restaurants, Ruby Chow's is located in a turn-of-the-century mansion . . . redecorated handsomely in red, black and gold Chinese motifs and enhanced with special pieces carved for Ruby in Hong Kong.

Ruby herself, complete to famous high-piled hairdo, will probably greet you. Husband, Ping, is Supreme Boss of the kitchen. If you are a connoisseur of Chinese food, you'll appreciate the variety and the care taken with each item. Among their more famous specialties are egg roll, Mandarin duck and shark's fins . . . but there are many, many more. Chinese music playing in the background adds to the atmosphere, too.

If your group orders one of the big, fancy Chinese dinners, you'll probably come to the conclusion that I have—that the Chinese must have invented feasts.

PORK FRIED RICE (serves 4)

2 T oil
½ c pork, chicken or shrimp, diced
1/4 small dry onion, diced
1 egg
2 c rice, cooked

1/4 t salt
½ t MSG
2 t soy sauce
1 stalk grn. onion, chopped
1/4 c lettuce, shredded

Brown diced meat and dry onion in hot oil in heavy skillet, then scramble egg with meat. Lower heat and add rice, salt, MSG and soy. Mix well. Mix in green onion and shredded lettuce. Serve immediately.

Brdwy & Jefferson
MA 2-6707
Mon-Fri
5 pm-1 am
Sat 6 pm-2 am
Cocktails
Sun 3 pm-11 pm
Dinners frm $2.95

167

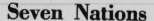

Seven Nations

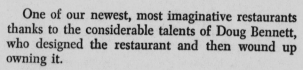

One of our newest, most imaginative restaurants thanks to the considerable talents of Doug Bennett, who designed the restaurant and then wound up owning it.

A short way from downtown, it commands a view of Elliott Bay which you may scarcely notice for looking around at the tasty details of the decor and enjoying the tasty details of your food.

You may be dining on beef Stroganoff or beef brochette, or might like to try tenderly treated seafoods, such as lobster, abalone or Hawaiian mahi mahi.

You'll be sitting in a very smart, contemporary setting. Walls are predominately pristine white, perfect foil for touches of rich, "hot" color motifs and the handsome pieces of native arts and crafts from the seven nations concerned. And if you phone ahead for a reservation, Doug will present you with a Seven Nations check for 10¢ to cover the cost.

OYSTERS FLORENTINE (serves 4)

1 pt oysters
2 lb. spinach, chopped
2 c cream sauce
1/4 c parmesan cheese

½ c liquor of oysters
2 oz. parmesan cheese
2 oz. melted butter

Poach oysters in very little liquid. Cook spinach in water left on from washing. Lay oysters on bed of spinach in individual shells. Cover with Mornay sauce; sprinkle with rest of cheese. (Sauce: 2 c cream sauce, ½ c oyster liquor, 2 oz. parm. cheese stirred into hot sauce; 2 oz. butter added at last.)

208 Elliott W
AT 2-2560
Mon-Fri
11:30-12m
Sat 5:30-12 m
Cocktails
Dinners frm $3.50

Snoqualmie Falls Lodge

This one has been a tradition in our area ever since I can remember—and thanks to the new fast highway it now is only about a half-hour drive from the city center through some of the most pleasant mountain scenery we have to offer.

It is perched above our most important historic falls . . . and even if there is only a trickle of water over them during certain dry times of the year the long drop is breath-taking . . . and Orville Graves, a restaurant man of the Old School, knows how to provide properly-prepared food under relaxed and pleasant lodge-type atmosphere.

Pan-fried chicken, steaks and grilled salmon . . . and the honey for your home-made biscuits is spooned from a position three feet above the table (just dishing it out is not sporting enough).

The Sunday farm breakfast is good, plentiful and memorable to thousands of us.

SAUTE'ED SALMON (8 to 12 oz. per person)

Choose either a fillet or slice of salmon. Flour and place in lightly buttered skillet (preheated to medium low temperature). Squeeze juice of ½ lemon over the salmon. Cover skillet. Cook 4 to 6 minutes. Turn salmon and squeeze juice of ½ lemon. Cook 4 to 6 minutes. Serve with tartar sauce or your favorite fish sauce. Do not overcook.

Snoqualmie, Wn.
TU 8-2451
Feb. 22-Sept. 30
12n-9:30 pm
Cocktails
Sun 9 am-9 pm
Dinner frm $3.75

169

Steve's Gay Nineties

The greatest collection of Northwest memorabilia has been made to live and breathe again here . . . stair cases from our fine old mansions . . . chandeliers from our old opera house . . . and the one I love best—the elegant back bar the "Feds" didn't have the heart to destroy during their frequent raids on the "speakeasies" during prohibition.

From the standpoint of decor of Flora Dora girls and of old Charlie Chaplin silent movies, the years drop off and the past appears. But the luxury-laden American buffet of 60 dishes is a tantalizing treat for very up-to-date appetites.

The entertainment is as authentic as the decor and strictly designed to prove that we enjoy fun and community singing accompanied by excellent food just as much as our forefathers. Lots of family parties earlier in the evening and on Sundays . . a more mature crowd later on when it's past the children's bed time.

South Tacoma
Seattle Phone
MA 2-4630
Tacoma Phone
GR 2-4471
7 Days, 24 hrs.
Cocktails
Entertainment
Dinners frm $2.25

OLD FASHIONED BAKED BEANS (serves 8)

4 c Great Northern beans 1/4 c table syrup
1 med. size onion,   ½ c catsup
  chopped   ½ c diced ham
1 t prepared mustard   ½ t kitchen bouquet

Cook beans in 10 cups salted water until done, but firm. Add ingredients and bake 3 hours.

Les Teagle's

A superior dinner house doing a superior job of providing the kind of food most often sought by the American people: steak and prime ribs.

A bright, clean, cozy, carpeted restaurant with impeccable table cloths and an equally impeccable view of Lake Union and the new freeway as it cuts along the west side of Capitol Hill. It's on a promontory on the east side of Aurora just as it rises from Mercer Street about 5 minutes from downtown.

The many repeat customers maintain that here are the friendliest waitresses in town, serving in addition to the food mentioned above, saute'ed crab legs with rice pilaff . . . small filets of sole, Amandine; fresh pork tenderloin . . . crab and shrimp Louie and Les Teagle's own salad dressings.

Generally a quietly sophisticated place with special emphasis on the prime ribs, which are better than any *you* could possibly obtain or prepare at home.

RICE CUSTARD PUDDING (serves 8)

8 eggs	Topping—
1 t vanilla	2 T butter
1½ qts milk	½ c brown sugar
½ c sugar	2 c corn flakes
pinch salt	2 T chopped walnuts
cooked rice	

Mix first 5 ingredients, pour into 8 individual cups over a small amount of rice. Set cups in pan of water, bake 325° for 45 min. Crunchy Topping: melt butter, add brown sugar and heat until bubbling. Add corn flakes, chopped walnuts, and turn out onto waxed paper to cool. Serve sprinkled over top of custards.

920 Aurora N
AT 4-7066
4:30 pm-
12:30 am
Cocktails
Dinners frm $3.65

Thunderbird

Just about the most unusual place to dine around Seattle is perched, literally, on top of a mountain peak one hour away. And the thrill begins with a chair-lift ride to get up the mountainside to the Thunderbird—there's no road; even the supplies ride the lift.

There's a dramatic effect approaching a double triangle building poised on concrete piers that lift it above winter's 20 ft. snowfalls. Orange-stained cedar walls loom above, the Thunderbird painted hugely on one. Inside is a sunken triangular fireplace surrounded by the dining room and immense view windows. Swiss fondue cookery is the cuisine accent . . . boeuf or cheese . . . deep dish apple pie . . . Thunderburgers.

The new Snoqualmie Skihaus at the base of the lift is the center of the area's family of buildings—offering lodging, food, ski equipment, and even interdenominational church services at the Chapel of St. Bernard.

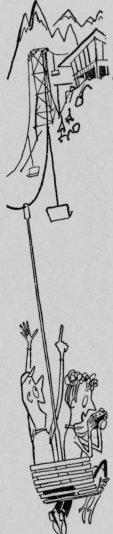

SNOQUALMIE DEEP DISH APPLE PIE
(Serves 6)

2 No. 2 cans sliced apples	pastry for one-crust pie
½ c sugar	1 c water
2 T cornstarch	1 c sugar
½ t cinnamon	1/4 lb. butter
½ t nutmeg	½ t rum flavor
4 T butter	½ t cinnamon
	½ t nutmeg
	2 T cornstarch

Mix first 6 ingredients in 8x8" baking pan. Top with pastry. Brush with canned milk. Bake 450° 10 min. then 350° 40 min. Cook last 7 ingredients until smooth and thickened (stir). Serve sauce over pie.

Snoqualmie Pass
EA 4-0514
10 am-4:30 pm
Wed Thur Sat Sun
During ski season
Dinners frm $2.85

Eye of the Needle*

The Space Needle is still completing its spectacular rise as we write, but we do know this—that the restaurant on top will command a fabulous view (two mountain ranges) and the management is such that we can look forward to a fine cuisine.

The Needle will be higher by 200-300 ft. than anything you can stand on in Seattle, unless you're a TV steeplejack. With its 60 ft. jet of gaslight on top, the Needle is about to become our No. 1 landmark unless Mt. Rainier looks to its laurels by erupting. And even then, you couldn't eat at the top of Rainier.

Decor is still jelling, but they've licked one basic: since the restaurant revolves once an hour, it will be divided into four identifying color sections. How would you like to be a waitress emerging from a kitchen to find your customers gone?

As we went to press, this name was changed from Top of the Needle to Eye of the Needle.

BAKED FILLET OF PUGET SOUND SALMON
(serves 6)

6 8 oz. fillets of salmon   Mixture of: salt, thyme
3 T butter for each fillet   and pepper

Turn seasoned fillets in butter melted in baking dish. Cover. Bake 350°, 30 min. Baste frequently. Dress fish on bed of Pilaf and top with onion and green pepper rings (fried) and pan juices reduced with 1 T white wine, 1 oz. sweet butter, touch lime juice. (Pilaf: Saute' ½ chopped onion, ½ lb. rice in 2 oz. butter a few minutes. Add 3 cups consomme, garni of 3 branches parsley, 1 branch thyme, 1 clove garlic, 1 bay leaf, salt and pepper. Bring to a boil, cover, reduce heat for 18 or 20 min. Fork in 1 oz. fresh butter.)

Address
(Just look up)
MU 2-7700
Noon-2 am
Cocktails
Open Sun
Dinners frm $3.75

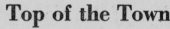

Top of the Town

Back in the days when potted palms, the string trio, and formal elegance marked the tradition of dining, we boarded the Madison Street cable car and dined at the Sorrento Hotel.

Today, there are no cable cars. But it's the Top of the Town, retaining the charm of the earlier part of the century—using cable car motifs on the menus and old time wrought iron chairs. And through the great windows high on First Hill, the decor is an excellent view of nowadays Seattle.

The old-fashioned menu has been streamlined to the point where one dinner item is served . . . and their specialty is really special. It's a prime rib dinner wheeled in and served with a flourish by the chef.

The Sorrento boasts another spot for dining—the new Dunbar Room at the Terry Ave. entrance. It's wonderfully old English with dark paneling, rich colored glass, and downright comfy.

Sorrento Hotel
Terry & Madison
MA 2-6400
5:30 pm-1 am
Cocktails
Dinner frm $3.95

BAKED POTATO *(per serving)*

1 12 or 14 oz. Idaho
    baking potato
3 pats butter (or 4)
2 t sour cream
2 t crisp bacon, chopped

1 t chives, chopped
2 t Parmesan cheese
salt, paprika, ground
    pepper

Bake potato in foil at 400° 1½ hours. Split open, add butter. Top with sour cream and rest of ingredients. Serve with prime rib beef with horseradish sauce. (½ grated horseradish and ½ whipped cream.)

Trader Vic's

You who come from Trader Vic towns know the joys of his special approach to Polynesian foods. Those of you who are unacquainted have a real delight in store.

The decor itself will lull you and enchant you first of all . . . with its thatching, and tiki gods, tropical plants and other exotic touches.

But even more, the gentle perfection that goes into the preparation of the dishes—served by almond-eyed personnel in South Seas-influenced costumes—will open your eyes to new flavors in familiar foods.

It is a Trader Vic conviction to serve fish gently cooked in wine sauces, meats barbecued in special Chinese ovens fed with alder wood only, fascinating soups, beautiful and exotic salads . . . and a host of fabulous and beautiful drinks that will convince you in no time at all that you are as good as in the languid South Seas.

WATER CHESTNUTS WITH CHICKEN LIVERS

soy sauce	chicken livers
fresh or canned water chestnuts	bacon, thin

Dip liver slices in soy sauce. Insert a slice of water chestnut between two slices of chicken liver (liver slices slightly larger than chestnut slices). Wrap with strip of bacon, skewer with a toothpick, and fry in deep fat 3 min. 375°. Serve as hors d'oeuvres.

5th & Virginia
MA 4-7400
10:30 am-lgl clsng
Cocktails
Dinners frm $4.00

Viceroy

If you have always secretly desired to make an impressive entrance into a cosmopolitan restaurant, then the Viceroy is for you.

A short flight of wide stairs descend into the main room and an atmosphere reminiscent of the Diamond Jim era of dining lengthily and well. Much use has been made of walnut paneling, silver candlesticks, chandeliers, deeply upholstered banquettes.

A very sophisticated spot with waiters and menu to match. Chicken saute' (sec) with wild rice. . . . broiled pepper steak risotto . . . rex sole saute' belle meuniere, just to mention a few.

Sophistication heightened by the real address, 1608 Times Court "Alley."

TOURNEDOS OF BEEF (serves 6)

6 rounds of toast
1 small can goose liver
   paste
6 filet mignon, broiled

6 tomato slices, fried in
   bread crumbs
2 c Sauce Bernaise

On one side of toast spread liver paste. Top with filet, tomato, Bernaise. (Sauce Bernaise: Beat 6 egg yolks over hot water in top of double boiler. Add 2 oz. burgundy, 1 tsp. tarragon vinegar, 1 tsp. tarragon, chopped fine. Beat fluffy. Add 1 cube unsalted butter and 2 cubes reg. butter (melted). Add one onion saute'ed with 1/4 lb. sliced mushrooms. (Stuffed zucchini and artichoke hearts served on the side.)

Westlake & Pine
MA 2-2106
11:30 am-lgl clsng
Cocktails
Entertainment
Dinners frm $3.75

176

Victor's 610 Pine

Padrone Victor Rosellini and partner John Poggetti recently lowered both the ceiling and the prices at the 610 Pine. It's a happy establishment, Victor's 610. There's a friendly family atmosphere about the place. The decor is gay Italo-French. Food and refreshments are first-cabin, always. Featured is a prix fixe $3.00 dinner served daily and on Sundays.

Luncheon and dinner menus are wide and varied, with a Florentine accent. Pogetti prepares chicken cacciatore, veal scaloppine, and the like in the classic manner. Victor's Special—a tasty blend of spinach, eggs and ground beef—is a favorite with the clientele.

Victor came to Seattle from Bimbo's in 1950, and John from Amelio's. If I have to tell you where those restaurants are, you wouldn't understand the importance of this part of their pedigrees, anyway!

BAKED LASAGNE (serves 8)

1/4 lb. beef	3 whole eggs
1/4 lb. veal	2 T parmesan cheese
1 whole onion	dash nutmeg
2 c cooked spinach	dash allspice
salt and pepper to taste	2 lb. lasagne

Combine first five ingredients. Cook tender, grind. Blend with eggs, 2 T parmesan, dash each of nutmeg and allspice. Cook lasagne in boiling, salted water. Layer lasagne and meat mixture in baking dish, starting with lasagne. Bake 350° 25 minutes.

610 Pine
MA 4-2355
11 am-legal clsng
Cocktails
Entertainment
Sun 4-10 pm
Dinners frm $3

Vito's

We have often referred to Vito's as "one of the best kept secrets in town" . . . so it's with pleasure we join the violently partisan "regulars" in helping to let the secret out.

Brothers Vito and Jimmy Santoro have developed a restaurant that is attractive, yet casual. They take turns at the bar, kidding the customers, unless, of course, the customers are kidding them.

They have a couple of important assets in chef Guido, who has his own way of performing miracles with Italian-style food . . . and in a lady who, among other culinary talents, makes their excellent pizza and blesses the dough, as she was taught in Italy when nine years old.

I am particularly fond of the lamb shanks . . . other favorites are veal parmigiana, saute'ed chicken livers with mushrooms, and pot roast with mostacciola.

LAMB SHANKS (serves 6)

6 lamb shanks	1 clove garlic
1 med. sized onion	olive oil
4 pieces celery	1½ c tomato puree
	2 c water

9th & Madison
MU 2-2695
9:30 am-lgl clsng
Cocktails
Dinners frm $3.75

Brown lamb shanks in olive oil. Add chopped vegetables, add tomato puree, water. Bake uncovered 400° 20 min.; 350° until done.

178

Von's

Tradition here is as long as the menu of over 300 items . . . Von's is the only one of the fine old Seattle restaurants of half a century ago that has survived prohibition . . . the Black Thirties . . . the bustling building program of a powerfully forging city.

Mostly Von's has gone to modern decor but hints of the Von's I remember as a kid may be found in the tiled entrance, the enormous counter, the huge plate glass mirror in the back bar. But the thing that has kept Von's favored all these years is still there —the fine and intriguing variety of foods.

Their clam chowder is proclaimed by many as the best in Seattle . . . also notable, their baked stuffed crab, their "sauce" dishes—Hungarian goulash, sauerbraten, mulligan stew, boiled beef— even these represent only a *soupcon* of the extensive cuisine. All available 24 hours a day.

MULLIGAN STEW (serves 6)

3 lbs. chuck beef
1 med. onion diced
5 potatoes cubed
5 carrots cubed

10 small pearl onions
1 c stewed tomatoes
burgundy

Braise onion in small amount of oil. Brown 1 inch squares of beef. Reduce heat and simmer slowly 1½ hours covered. Add water as needed. Add tomatoes, carrots. Cook ten minutes. Add potatoes and onions. When vegetables are done add a little flour to thicken. Add small amount burgundy wine.

1423 4th Ave
MA 3-4509
24 hrs-7 days
Cocktails
Dinners frm $2.75

And Further More ---

"The eating habits of our habitue's and sons of habitue's"

Outside of a dignified, intellectual discussion of the Freeway, Second Lake Bridge, fluoridation, politics or religion, the easiest way to get into an argument in Seattle is to take a position on where to buy your best meals.

So herewith are some other observations on places we've been and liked or heard about and liked what we heard:

For example, we were told by someone who was talking like he knew that the best two places in town for a good corned beef sandwich were the *Rainbow Club Cafe* on Pike Street and *Moe's Broiler* on Second Avenue. I'm not prepared to argue the matter because I never have been in either of these places —and the gentleman who was passing along the information was their supplier. But we're a city loaded with connoisseurs of corned beef and it might be that a little intellectual discussion could be stirred up on this subject.

And after that one you could toss an egg in the fan by bringing up the matter of Chinese restaurants. For some reason everybody is an expert on this one, but practically nobody can come to terms on which is the best "find" in town. In addition to those mentioned, I happen to be partial to *Tai Tung* in the International Settlement and most especially to the *Jade Pagoda* up on Broadway East.

We sort of think of the latter as a "neighborhood" restaurant, but a little bit more of the world is beating a pathway to its door because of its egg-roll, boned chicken in sweet and sour sauce and the Chinese peapods.

We're great fish and seafood diners, too. I'm happy to state the old Indian habit of making a necklace of clams to hang around the neck when you're taking a long trip has disappeared from the scene. There are more pleasant ways of eating clams than munching one from time to time as you trot along the trail.

However, we'll frequently be found standing in line at the *Cove*, which is new and out on a dock with an interesting view, . . . *Crawfords*, which enjoys an unsurpassed view of the Empire Builder headed east, the Sound and the Olympics (weather permitting), and the *Wharf* where gather tourists by the thousands to admire the biggest fishing fleet in the United States (1,000 boats) right out in the middle of Fishermen's Terminal.

We have a lot of people who "eat" through one of these restaurant books with pencil and black notebook in hand (and poison pen at home which is used on me if they happen to disagree with my observations.)

But here are some thoughts for you explorers: *Lee's* in the University District for an exquisite decor and continental type food . . . *Simpson's* on Roy Street off Broadway—say on Sunday for that delightful leg of lamb . . . *Lowell Dining Room* to check out the soup and dessert . . . *Bel Terrace,* try the Factoria Overpass to 118 S.E. in Bellevue on the north side of the Sunset Highway . . . but also try ringing them ahead for a reservation. They like preparing the food especially for *you.*

Most of the rest of Alki Point where our founding fathers "founded" us has been forgotten, but not the *Alki Homestead* which is in a log "mansion" and the chicken on Sunday is served family style if you have a family. Our small daughter just dies over the hamburgers at the *Plaid Piper* on Capitol Hill, but I'm partial to the martinis and memories of their very secluded cocktail lounge. People in Bellevue keep telling me the pies at the *Village Inn* are just as good as they used to be . . . And the other night Shirley and I ran across the *Bistro* on Roosevelt Way. Operated by Matts and Siri Djos, how could it be anything but casually continental and very intime for the intimately inclined?

My visits to the *Flame* in Kirkland have been pleasantly hectic memories of a lot of fun after we have driven across the lake to have lunch there with friends, gone by boat to the U.W. Football Stadium, which is about 8 blocks north of our house, returned to the *Flame* by boat for more jolly conversation and then driven the 15 miles back to our house.

Our very competent spies, who have more money for dining out than we do, keep an alert eye on the *Moscow* restaurant, which was moved out to Houghton by the new freeway . . . and the *Troyka* on North 45th. Both are serving excellent Russian food. They report that the only good Turkish food in town is to be found at *Tacher's* in the Pike Place Market . . . that

181

Maneki's—long time favorite of local and visiting Japanese—is working on a decor to match its excellent menu . . . that *Campo's* in the University District is a bit of Mexican atmosphere (with a Texas influence) . . . that *A La Petite France* is forging ahead as a typical small French restaurant on a modest scale . . . that the decor in the *Schnitzelhaus* (obviously German) is not to "die over" but they have dandy potato pancakes, German music and posters, the latest German language newspapers, and German customers who like the way my German grandmother cooked.

Little Reasons Why We Like It Here . . .

For that luscious pie at the *Green Apple Pie* which will pass the 2 million home-baked pie mark in 1962 . . . For *Daverso's* pizza down on Pioneer Square . . . For the hot pastrami sandwiches and cheesecake at the *Hot Pastrami* . . . For the home made desserts at *Vicky's Lazy Susan* in Bellevue . . . For the Kansas corn-fed beef and the imported San Francisco sour-dough French bread at *Angelo's* in Burien . . .

For Swedish pancakes at the *Scandia Bakery* . . . For the *Stalder's* Special sandwich featuring 5 kinds of meat and 2 kinds of cheese on lovely rich bread . . . For the hamburgers at the *Jolly Boy* in Renton . . .

For the "pasties" (Welsh meat pies) at the *Chanticleer* just across the Ballard Bridge . . . For the late night snacks at *Elroy's* who has rejuvenated an old Pioneer Square landmark and helped it to live again . . . For the prime ribs of beef at the *Brigadier Room*.

Because of the originality of some of our pizza places, like *Pizza Pete* who advertises "pizza to go" with a discus thrower poised with pizza in hand . . . because the original *Pancake House* is in the Pacific Northwest (Portland, we hate to admit) . . . and we've got our share of these pleasant places.

For dandy places to have a reason to "go to" out of the city like the *Shorline* in Gig Harbor or the *Hearthstone* in Bremerton . . . both very swank and pleasant restaurants in unbelievably beautiful view settings . . . the laughter-filled *Bavarian* in Tacoma serving excellent German food along with fun, beer and German music . . . and the *Seahorse* in Mukilteo, famous for its Captain's Table Smorgasbord on Wednesday.

Index

Restaurants

Adolfo's 127
Andy's Diner 128
Bib 'N Tucker 129
Bob's Landing 130
Bryan's Lake Terrace 131
Bull 'N Bear 132
Bush Garden 133
Canlis 134
Captain's Table 135
Casa Villa 136
Cascade Room 137
Cloud Room 138
Crabapple 139
Dublin House 140
El Gaucho 141
Eye Of The Needle..............173
Four Winds 142
Franco's Hidden Harbor........143
Frederick and Nelson...........144
French Quarter 145
Golden Lion 146
Grove 147
Harold's Satellite 148
Hilton Inn 149
Hofbrau 150
Hong Kong 151
Hyatt House 152
Ivar's Acres Of Clams 153
Johnny's Dock 154
Kalua Room 155
King Oscar's 156
Lakewood Terrace 157
Legend Room 158
Nikko 159
Nisco's 160
Norselander 161
Pancho's 162
Polynesia 163
Red Carpet 164
Roma 165
Rosellini's Four-10 166
Ruby Chow's 167
Seven Nations 168
Snoqualmie Falls Lodge 169
Steve's Gay Nineties 170
Les Teagle's 171
Thunderbird 172
Top Of The Town 174
Trader Vic's 175
Viceroy 176
Victor's 610 Pine 177
Vito's 178
Von's 179

Recipes

Apple Pie, Deep Dish 172
Beans, Baked 170
Beef, Boiled In Pot 147
Beef, Bunlay Strips 140
Beef, Ground Sirloin 128
Beef Stroganoff 162
Beef, Tournedos 176
Cheese Cake 131
Chicken, Bavarian En Casserole..156
Chicken Cacciatore 136
Chicken Dore, Kiev 166
Chicken, Kamaaina 155
Chicken Saute' Sec 127
Chicken Wrapped In Paper 163
Chop Suey, Almond Chicken ...151
Cocotte De Poulette Au Vin 157
Crab and Cheese Soup 138
Crab, Deviled Au Gratin 142
Crab Legs, Dungeness 143
Crab Ravessant 144
Crab Salad, Baked 137
French Dressing, Canlis 149
Halibut, Poached In Wine 130
Lamb Shanks 178
Lasagne, Baked 177
Lobster Tails En Brochette 146
Lobster Thermidor 161
Mulligan Stew 179
Oysters Florentine 168
Pesto Ala Genovese 165
Pork Fried Rice 167
Potato, Baked 174
Potato Dumplings, German 150
Rice Custard Pudding 171
Roquefort Cheese Cream
    Dressing 164
Roquefort Cheese Dressing 148
Salad, Greek Goddess 132
Salmon, Fillet 173
Salmon, Poached Au Riesling....154
Salmon Sakamushi 159
Salmon, Saute'ed 169
Sandwich, Mr. Bellevue 139
Sauce, Fermiere 135
Scallops and Mushrooms 158
Shish Kebob El Gaucho 141
Shrimp, Canlis' 134
Shrimp Curry, Hawaiian 129
Sole Mornay, Fillets 153
Sukiyaki, Mr. Seko 133
Tripe, Saute'ed 145
Water Chestnuts & Chicken
    Livers 175
Veal Cutlet, Gentilhomme 152
Veal Scaloppine 160

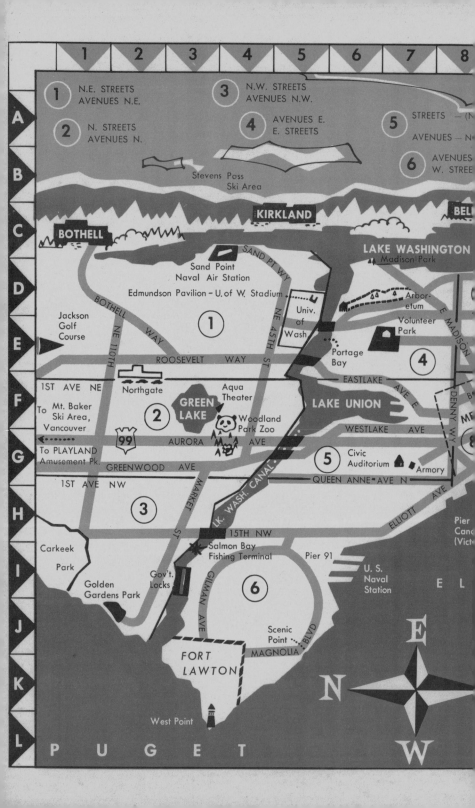